Bare Bones

*What an Orthopedic Surgeon Worries About
With Respect to Childhood Injury*

Jordan Paynter, MD

Paynter Books, LLC

Bare Bones: What an Orthopedic Surgeon Worries About With Respect to Childhood Injury

Copyright © 2024 by Jordan Paynter, MD

All rights reserved.

Printed in the United States of America. All rights reserved. Except as permitted under the United States Copyright Act of 1976, no part of this book may be reproduced in any form or by any electronic or mechanical means, including information storage and retrieval systems, without written permission from the author, except for the use of brief quotations in a book review.

Disclaimer: The advice and strategies found within may not be suitable for every situation. This work is sold with the understanding that neither the author nor the publisher are held responsible for the results accrued from the advice in this book.

1st Edition.

ISBN 13: 978-8-21854629-8

ISBN-10: 8-21854629-8

Published by Paynter Books, LLC through Kindle Direct Publishing.

To my loving wife, thank you for being so supportive and doing the lion's share of raising our children. I honestly couldn't do it without you!

To my sister Emily and my father Steve, thank you for your time spent editing.

To my own mother Judy, thank you for keeping me alive.

To my editor Savanna, thank you for helping me with this project on top of your already full schedule.

Contents

Foreword	vii
1. Introduction	1
2. Bones	8
3. Learning from Injuries	16
4. Death Statistics	38
5. Automobiles	53
6. Swimming Pools and Drowning	76
7. Other Vehicles	89
8. Falls	103
9. Trampolines and Playgrounds	109
10. Choking	116
11. Poison and Ingestion	129
12. Firearms	139
13. Fire Danger	151
14. Homicide/Child Abuse	157
15. Suicide	165
16. Traumatic Brain Injury and Spinal Cord Injury	175
17. Lightning Strikes	187
18. Animals and Allergies	191
19. Deaths in the Developing World	208
20. Summary	213
21. Injury Appendix: What To Do	217
22. Notes	242
Stay Connected!	249

Foreword

Allow me to introduce myself: my name is Jordan Paynter, and I am an orthopedic surgeon. If you're unfamiliar with my profession, I am a medical doctor who specializes in both surgical and non-surgical treatment of muscles, bones, and joints. I am married to the most wonderful woman I could have imagined, and we have been blessed with four beautiful children. It is primarily because of my wife I am writing this book.

My wife and I are complete opposites in many respects. Anyone who knows us could tell you I am generally a laid-back person, almost to a fault in my personal life outside of my work (this excludes driving and Georgia football). My wife, on the other hand, is not. She typically carries a lot of anxiety about daily happenings, which is probably one of the reasons we work so well together. We balance each other. She is an excellent planner and organizer, which keeps us on time. She has a degree in early childhood education and knows a lot more than me about childhood development. However, she often gets worried about medical issues and has no background in knowing when to be legitimately concerned and when not to be worried,

Foreword

particularly when it comes to our children. I, on the other hand, have a different set of concerns with our children because of my training.

I have a medical degree and grew up in a family of medical providers while my wife did not. Since my mother is a nurse and my father is a physician, my mindset toward medical maladies has always been affected by their backgrounds and methods of dealing with those maladies. They provided knowledge and experience. They used it well to care for my sisters and me, and they imparted it to me. This familiarity with healthcare led to my interest in medicine as a career. In the same vein, my dad was the one I called for medical advice prior to becoming a physician myself. My wife, however, does not come from a healthcare-centered background with regard to her family. Because of our stark differences in our approach and upbringing with regard to medical problems, it struck me just how little the average person typically learns about the human body, the way it injures, and the way it heals. Now, my wife has the advantage (and often nuisance!) of being married to a physician, yet she still has anxiety about potential illnesses and injuries with our children. She and I even get into light-hearted jests about how to approach medical illnesses.

When thinking about certain career advantages, I am reminded of the board game *Life*. You pick a career early in the game and benefit at times throughout gameplay. For instance, if you choose mechanic as your career, landing on a space that causes your car to break down is advantageous because you can fix it yourself. However, if you go see a movie, you have to pay. Likewise, if you choose to be an actor, you have to pay to fix your car but not to go see a movie. My upbringing led me to choose being a physician as a career, and I recognize the advantage my education provides for dealing with medical scenarios. My purpose for *Bare Bones* is to provide insights and advice to those who do not have healthcare training or a reliable medical influence.

My wife often imagines detailed scenarios about how our child could be seriously injured while doing a certain activity, such as

Foreword

jumping on a trampoline, riding a bike, swimming, even eating. I tend to object to these scenarios. I am quick to admit I am not all knowing, but I strive to take an evidenced-based approach to sorting out medical fact from medical fiction. Medical school does more than just teach medical fact; it teaches how to approach knowledge and learn new information because the medical field is always changing. We are taught to use an evidence-based approach to ensure we are performing the appropriate research before making decisions, and you'll find that approach as the basis of this book.

Additionally, my wife invents death scenarios for our children rivaling those of the *Final Destination* movies. I am sure many parents regularly find themselves in the same experience. Having children is the most insanely anxiety-provoking life event I have experienced, and I am not a naturally anxious person. While I generally do not worry about most parts of life, after having our first son, it suddenly hit me how mortal I was and what true fear felt like. Serious injury or death to my children is my single largest fear in life. A close second is the same happening to my wife, and that fear has only strengthened with each child because I could not imagine doing life or parenting without her. While I don't dwell on these hypothetical scenarios, my wife has helped me realize how easy it is for seemingly improbable thoughts to quickly spiral, resulting in more stress around an already difficult job as a parent.

The first goal of *Bare Bones* is to establish my background as a physician and relay my training and experiences as an orthopedic surgeon to explain my views on childhood injuries. Subsequently I will discuss why children are so well equipped to deal with injury. I will then review the leading causes of death in children in modern times.

This brings me to the final goal of the book: how to keep children safe. My wife and I have the same fears for our children, but mine result from statistics and experience as a medical provider. Her fears rest around what she reads and hears about: anecdotes, headlines, and social media. The things I get highly anxious about are securing

Foreword

the car seat and swimming pools. Particularly with the car seat, my wife and I debate how tight to make the harness. We work well together as a team because we balance each other out and focus on different concerns. Together, we want to keep our children safe and alive. My hope with the second topic is to direct parental anxiety toward realistic major risks so you can focus your attention on the things that matter rather than getting lost in the weeds. It's difficult to enjoy time with your children when focusing on all of the what ifs. There is a good balance between healthy concern and true pathologic anxiety, and if I can provide education on a few topics, I hope to ease your general fears as a non-medical parent and instead direct your attention to the relatively small number of actual concerns affecting children.

Of course, raising a child is much more than just keeping them alive. It involves all sorts of other complex issues and psychological challenges. I will not pretend to be an expert on that, and it will remain outside the scope of this book.

Lastly, I must make a disclaimer. Although I am a medical doctor, I am not giving you specific medical advice for your situation or telling you how to approach specific injuries with your child. I am trying to impart general knowledge in a fun way so you can have a better frame of reference when approaching medical maladies and appropriately focus your attention on how to keep your children safe from harm. This does not substitute for a medical visit with a medical provider. In an emergency, you should always seek care immediately, and call your medical provider if you are concerned for the medical wellbeing of your child.

Additionally, some of the views presented in this book are my personal opinion based on experience and data review. I will try to point out specific recommendations by our medical organizations where appropriate and highlight where my personal opinions differ. My goal is to raise awareness.

Chapter 1

Introduction

Many people wonder what physicians worry about. Physicians seem to be at the center point of a lot of entertainment, namely in the form of TV. My wife used to frequently watch the show *Grey's Anatomy*. While I was in medical school, I found myself scoffing at stuff I overheard while she was watching and would often try to tell my wife how unrealistic certain scenarios were in the show. There are many other television series that have captivated the attention of countless viewers, but you will rarely find a medical doctor who watches such shows. Most of us are like this because we get hung up on details.

Becoming a medical doctor requires a high amount of intelligence, but I have found the best physicians do not only have a high knowledge base but also know how to use common sense to apply that knowledge toward the goal of helping a person in need. In other words, being a great physician requires taking what you know and rationally applying it. This process takes years of training and experience and does not really ever end.

The second quality that makes a great physician, in my opinion, is being able to take the information that you know and summarize it in a way that can be used to successfully educate a patient. I'm sure many readers feel the same: the best doctors are the ones who can explain things to you in a way that you can quickly and easily understand.

For those of you who are not quite sure how medical training works, it depends on the specialty. In the United States, entering medical school requires an undergraduate degree. All physicians must then complete a four-year medical school education (although some schools have trended toward three) and then do a period of intense specialty training called *residency*. The term *residency* arose because in the past, resident physicians spent so much time at the hospital they might as well have lived there. Fortunately, it is somewhat better nowadays, but most residencies are still incredibly grueling and require an amount of dedication that few can understand without having witnessed it. For orthopedic surgery, you must complete a five-year residency after your four years of medical school. That's nine years of training after completing an undergraduate degree. Most orthopedic surgeons do a sixth year, called a *fellowship*, for subspecialty training. For orthopedics, the common subspecialties include: hand surgery, joint replacement surgery, shoulder surgery, sports medicine, spine surgery, pediatric orthopedics, and foot and ankle surgery. That is ten years of postgraduate education before you step into the "real world" on your own. Medical school tends to be more like other forms of schooling requiring lectures and grades, but residency is a wild combination of self-directed studying and the hardest job you could imagine in the form of an apprenticeship (all while getting paid pretty poorly on top of that).

My subspecialty training is actually *not* in pediatric orthopedics. I am subspecialty trained in adult reconstruction, or hip and knee replacement surgery. The field of pediatric orthopedics is typically more reserved for advanced pediatric limb deformities, scoliosis of the spine, and the treatment of limb maladies associated with congenital problems such as cerebral palsy and other neurological disorders. All orthopedic surgeons, regardless of subspecialty training, are well trained in residency to treat common childhood fractures and injuries. In my personal practice, I do more than just hip and knee replacements. I see other ailments on the orthopedic spectrum, and I treat a fair number of pediatric fractures. Children are some of the most rewarding patients to treat because children generally heal extremely well because of their awesome growth potential. One of the sayings we commonly used in residency was "children are lizards" because they seem to be able to heal some of the most severe limb trauma fairly well.

So why am I qualified to write this book? I am a practicing orthopedic surgeon with experience in treating children, but I am also the father of many young children, three boys and a new baby girl to be precise. My wife is not medically trained and often sees the world differently from me. That combination gives me a worldview of personal experience as a parent, personal experience as a physician who treats childhood injury, and personal experience with someone I dearly love who does not have the same medical background.

One of the most common responses I see to childhood injury on the parent's end is panic. Many people don't know what an emergency is and what is not. The issue tends to be the *concern* of the parent, and often my job is to reassure patients' parents that their child will be fine. Parents love their children and do not want to see them harmed. When we see our child hurt, we tend to hurt with them and for them because of our love. While we parents fear bodily injury to our children, I think it is important to recognize the difference between a relatively minor injury and what can lead to permanent disability or death. Many parents do not know what activities or parts of their day put their children at the highest risk. Some of us can get so lost in the weeds of watching our children closely during playtime on the playground, but we forget to properly secure our children when we get into a vehicle on a daily basis. Many are not up to date on the appropriate safety measures for children, such as when they can use certain booster seats. I've seen firsthand the disastrous consequences of failing to properly secure a child in a vehicle, and it's not something I want for my children.

The purpose of this book is to redirect parental focus on things that are at the highest risk of posing serious harm or even death to your child so that you may appropriately take steps to keep your child safer. I will focus on children aged 10 and under but will include older ages where appropriate. Additionally, my hope is that this will reduce your anxiety when it comes to most of your daily routine with the knowledge of the real risks so that you may calm your mind during less dangerous activities.

In order to accomplish this, I will first give a background on what bones are, how they heal, and how my experiences as an orthopedic surgeon have taught me about the amazing capability of a child to heal from physical injury. Next, I will provide a chapter discussing statistical causes of death for children at certain age groups, drawing attention to the differences in medical disease-related versus injury-related causes of death. During this chapter, I will elaborate on the top 5 causes of preventable death caused by injury with the goal of raising your awareness of the true dangers to your child's life. Subsequently, I will provide multiple chapters on the top statistical dangers to children and how to take reasonable precautions to prevent them. I will discuss "child proofing" and preventative measures. Some of these categories will prove to be nearly completely preventable with a few simple rules while others will require more regular attention for maximal efficacy. Afterward, we will discuss traumatic brain injury and spinal cord injury, as these can cause permanent disability to children despite the child remaining alive. I will also spend a chapter pointing out the differences in childhood deaths in the developed world versus deaths in children in the developing or "third" world. I included a chapter on less common sources of death in children, such as animal bites and lightning strikes. Finally, I will provide a quick tips appendix chapter on how to initially deal with certain scenarios, such as what to do if you think your child has broken a bone or needs stitches.

Ultimately, my hope is that upon completing this book, you will have a better understanding of what poses significant risk of death or permanent disability to your child so that you can focus your attention on the deadliest things. Rather than using anecdotes or rare scenarios that you might catch in a headline, I will use statistical sources, and I will explain where I find the statistics and include references. In healthcare, we call this *evidence-based medicine*. To make the best and most informed decisions, we like to have well researched evidence to guide us in our respective fields. This includes going through multiple resources to come to appropriate conclusions. I am going to bring this approach to this book and provide the sources. If I can at least draw your attention to one risk you might not have thought of, then reading this book will have been worth it. In the same vein, if I can reduce your anxiety by calling attention to the most important risks that you can control so you don't feel overwhelmed, I will also consider that a success. Use this book as a reference to hopefully make parenting overall less stressful so you can enjoy the parts of it that will bring you joy.

There are two ways you could choose to read this book. You could read it cover to cover, or you could skip through for the sections you find most interesting, helpful, or relevant. This book can be read both ways. You do not have to read it in order, and you do not have to read every chapter to gain something useful. Some of the chapters may cover material that seems second nature to you because you've already done thorough child-proofing while others may teach you things you did not know.

I will cite many resources in this book, but I will highlight a few of the more common ones up front. The Center for Disease Control (CDC) tracks data from the U.S. yearly and publishes it for open access. This includes death and injury statistics, so I will refer to their database a lot in this book. *UpToDate* is a paid subscription service for medical providers with medical topics that are frequently updated with new research and recommendations. Think of it like an elite physician's version of Wikipedia, but with medical doctors providing background information with excellent citations. I rely on them heavily for parts of the book to keep up with the newest recommendations and facts. The American Academy of Pediatrics (AAP) is a large body of pediatricians that does a lot of excellent research on child health and injury. They publish some of the best reviews on safety and injury topics for children, so I will cite their resources and publications many times throughout this book. The AAP has a partner website called www.healthychildren.org, which is a fantastic resource for parents to review.

As I stated earlier, I am a practicing orthopedic surgeon and I routinely treat common children's fractures. I am not a pediatric orthopedic specialist nor am I a pediatric trauma surgeon, but I spent a lot of time in my residency training working with specialists from those fields, and I learned a lot about treatments of more severe injuries and non-orthopedic injuries. Also, part of our medical school education and residency education is heavily invested in reviewing research and learning how to interpret data and conclusions, including critiques of the studies themselves. I am well trained in interpreting research and applying it logically to situations, but also in picking out flaws in research design or interpretation. One caution is to understand that I myself am subject to bias, but I will try to keep things honest with the goal of showing what the research supports with regard to death and injury in children. I am also a parent with young children, so I have experience with daily issues that arise naturally from raising small children. Therefore, I have both a parental and physician outlook on how things work. I have witnessed firsthand the extremes of childhood injury and routinely treat common injuries. I also have a lot of personal experience with my own children sustaining mild injuries and the ways in which they put themselves in danger.

So here's your chance to know what makes an orthopedic surgeon worry in regards to children's injuries. This is going to be a combination of experience and well researched statistics to show what goes on in my world and in my head on a regular basis. Broken bones don't phase me because they are very treatable and only rarely cause a permanent problem. Certain situations make me more nervous than others. Hopefully this is a useful glance into the head of a physician.

Chapter 2

Bones

I've heard it said many times that if you're going to write something, write what you know. Well, I'm an orthopedic surgeon, and I know bones. Bones are a remarkable organ, and my treatment of orthopedic injuries has shaped my medical understanding of the body and my respect for how wonderful the human body really is. My goal with this chapter is to provide a background discussion on how bone healing works, particularly in children, and to express how remarkable the healing potential of a child can be. I will try not to make this like a biology textbook and instead keep it short and simple. Simply put, children have more of a knack for breaking bones than adults, but they also recover much quicker. In this chapter, I will cover the structure of bone, the common types of cells in bone, the way bones grow, growth plates, and define the word "fracture."

I recognize that many people are not into background information and just want to get to the meat of the book. Others find the details fascinating and want to learn. If you like details, then this chapter is for you. My intention is not to bore you, especially right off the bat, so feel free to skim or skip this chapter if you're not a *back-*

ground info sort of person. If you try to read this chapter and get bored and are thinking about putting the book down, skip to the next chapter.

What are bones?

Bones are often compared to pieces of wood. They are sturdy but can break and splinter. The truth is, they are much more sophisticated than the common tree branch. They are mostly composed of hydroxyapatite and collagen. Hydroxyapatite is the calcium part of the bone which forms a crystal structure and gives bone its compressive strength, or the ability to resist your weight while you walk. The collagen is the part that gives bone its tensile strength, or its ability to resist bending. Unlike non-living hard structures, however, bones can remodel, meaning they adapt to forces over time and change their shape in response to those forces.

There are two major groups of bones: flat bones and long bones. Flat bones consist of the bones of the skull, the pelvis, and the scapula (shoulder blade). Long bones are the bones of the limbs, such as the femur (thigh bone), the tibia (shin bone), humerus (arm bone), etc. As an orthopedist, I mostly deal with long bones, and since we are talking about limb injuries, long bones are most relevant when talking about kids. Long bones and flat bones have slightly different structures and ways of forming, so I will mostly discuss long bones to illustrate the points in this chapter.

Bones are three-dimensional structures. If you were to cut one in half and view the cross-section, the outer part, or rim, would look like a thick white line, and the inner part would resemble a sponge. The outer part is called the cortex, or *cortical bone*, and is what makes bone hard. The inner part is called the medullary canal and is made of softer bone material called *cancellous bone*. If you're a sushi person, think of the outer rim of rice being the cortex and the inner portion with the fish and vegetables being the medullary canal. Bone marrow resides in the medullary canal. Bone marrow is responsible for the creation of new blood cells, which is another wonderful function of bones.

How do bones work?

Bones have two major types of cells, osteoblasts and osteoclasts. They essentially work in response to the surrounding chemical and mechanical environment to remodel bone. Osteoclasts remove sections of bone that the osteoblasts will then replace. This provides bone the ability to change its shape, and ultimately remain strong. Think of this as a gardener tending a garden by removing excess crops. If you have too dense of a crop, it may smother some of the plants, so the gardener removes even healthy plants at times to allow better overall growth. Bone remodels itself in response to chemical signals, mechanical signals, and even electrical signals within the body. An example of bone changing in response to a chemical signal would be the body's use of hormones to regulate calcium levels in the body. Bone acts as a reservoir of calcium, and if more calcium is needed because of a drop in the amount of calcium circulating in your blood, the body can signal through a hormone pathway to increase the breakdown of bone to free up calcium.

The ability of bone to remodel in response to a mechanical signal is what makes it such a unique organ. A mechanical signal is simply a force, such as walking, that puts pressure directly on the bone structure. This is not as a result of something within the body but rather an external force. It's absolutely fascinating. We refer to this response as *Wolff's Law*. The bone will grow and strengthen in response to load, or essentially pressure that you exert on the bone. Put another way, "use it or lose it." If you were to lay in bed for two months, your bone would start to lose its strength and normal appearance. I see this on x-rays sometimes when treating adult injuries with prolonged periods where we do not allow people to walk or bear weight on their legs, for example. We refer to this appearance as "disuse osteopenia"; the bone is literally weakened when it is not used. Likewise, bone grows heavily in response to the way you use it. Children, for example, start with bowed legs but they straighten as children grow and use their legs for walking and running. For the healing pathway in children, bone can remodel from a crooked angle to straighten with time as the child continues to use the limb. In adult healing, the initial healing bone is disorganized and relatively weak, but the bone is slowly strengthened with time through the mechanical use of the limb to return to its original strength.

Cartilage

Bone starts as cartilage when you are in the womb. Cartilage is a structure somewhat similar to bone but generally softer and more flexible. There are multiple types of cartilage, and some structures remain cartilage permanently for supporting function. Ears, for example, remain cartilage throughout life so they can remain flexible. Cartilage caps exist at the end of bones to form joints because cartilage is softer and does better with friction than bone which allows for smooth motion. Developmentally, it makes sense that a fetus would have only cartilage at first. It allows them to be flexible in such a tight space. Some of the cartilage is replaced with bone by birth, but the majority is still very soft cartilage or soft bone to allow for the infant to be born from a tight space and through a tight space where a high amount of flexibility is required.

Think back to your own child or another baby. Newborns have weird looking limbs. Their shins are generally curvy, almost to the point where they look like a pair of parentheses. Their skulls can have odd appearances after birth pressure. If babies could magically walk at birth, they would look like little goblins with extremely bowed legs walking on the outside edges of their feet. You will also remember how crawling, standing, cruising, and walking are typically distinct processes that take time to develop. Infants' and toddlers' bones develop in response to those forces so that the legs are less bowed by the time they are approximately 12-18 months old. This correction happens because of the normal forces signaling to the bones that they would do best to straighten if they are to work efficiently based on the pattern of movement required by the body. By age 24 months, the angles of the knee are typically close to neutral. Then children will develop "knock knees" that peak around age 3 to 4 and then they will progress to a normal knee angle by around age 7. The final angle of the knee has a slight "knock knee" angle to it.

In pediatric orthopedic clinics during residency training, one of the common visits was for children with bowed legs. The vast majority of these were normally developing children around 18 months old with concerned caretakers. I spent a good bit of time in residency explaining to caretakers that it is normal for most children to look like this, and there's a range of "normal." There are some uncommon disorders of the limbs that cause problematic extreme angles of the limbs that sometimes require bracing and/or surgery, but thankfully these are rare.

Periosteum

Last but certainly not least is the periosteum. The word *periosteum* is Latin for "around the bone." (Honestly, we physicians are not that clever at naming things. Basically, we describe the structure, translate the words to Latin, and it makes it sound much fancier than it really is. Fun trick, right?) The periosteum is present on all bones, but illustrations of anatomy that the general public sees almost never include it. It is dried out and gone by the time fossils are made into skeletal displays. The periosteum is basically a soft tissue covering that envelops the majority of the bone, excluding the sections of bone in the joints. It is an extremely important part of bone structure and function. It provides blood flow to bones and contains a large amount of stem cells. As children grow, the periosteum provides bone the ability to grow wider (not longer - that's the growth plate described in the next section). In both children and adults, the periosteum provides the stem cells needed to heal the bone. In children, the periosteum is much thicker than in adults. This is one of the reasons children have a quicker and better bone healing response than adults. We do not need to go much more in depth into the basic science of bone structure for our purposes here.

Growth Plates

Growth plates were an enigma to me growing up because people would often mention old wives' tales about injuring growth plates by participating in too many sports or heavy sporting activities. Generally speaking, I think most people do not know what they are or how they work. Growth plates are essentially gaps in the bone where there is cartilage rather than bone. The "doctor word" for growth plate is *physis* (F-eye-sis). There are two growth plates in each long bone, one at either end. The cartilage cells in the growth plate start increasing in number in response to certain chemical signals, then they get larger. The cells die and release calcium. These areas are then calcified and turned from cartilage structure into bone. It is a fascinating process, and it is how all our limbs lengthen.

Growth plates can easily become injured because they are typically the weakest part of the bone. Most growth plate injuries are due to fractures, and the worse you injure the growth plate, the higher chance there is of either partial or full shutdown. This can certainly be detrimental, and pediatric orthopedists can help when this unfortunate event happens, but this is very rare. The vast majority of growth plate injuries do not stop growth of the child, particularly if they are appropriately treated. Most fractures in children are caused by falls from ground level, and these are very rarely severe enough to stop growth. Can children or adolescents injure their growth plates from overuse and permanently alter themselves? In general, the answer is no for normal activities like running or weightlifting. There are specific circumstances where you can injure the growth plate and cause cessation of growth, or at least alter it. Two common ones would be *Gymnast's Wrist* and *Little Leaguer's Shoulder*.

Gymnast's Wrist, or *Distal Radial Physeal Stress Syndrome*, (On second thought let's just stick with *Gymnast's Wrist*) occurs in children that are heavily involved with gymnastics. This is an injury to the growth plate of the wrist because the wrist is not a weight-bearing bone and is not built for that kind of stress, but gymnasts often use their arms as weight-bearing limbs. *Little Leaguer's Shoulder* occurs from overuse from pitching, usually in boys. This is most common in ages 10-12 and can alter the growth plate in the humerus (upper arm bone) near the shoulder. Efforts to raise awareness of this injury have increased, particularly with pitch count limits based on age to prevent this injury. Both of these are easily cured by stopping the activity entirely.

Can an orthopedist or radiologist (medical doctor specially trained in reading x-rays, MRIs, and other medical imaging) tell how much growth you have left by looking at X-rays of your bones? Yes, we actually can to a certain extent. General orthopedists view thousands of x-rays, so we become experienced in "eyeballing" how open the growth plate looks in a child and can at least say if the child is close to completion of growth. It is important for orthopedists to know whether a child's growth plates are still open because it can impact surgical treatment for certain injuries. For example, if the growth plates are still open during Anterior Cruciate Ligament (ACL) reconstruction surgery of the knee, it changes the surgical approach because drilling through the growth plate can be risky in a younger patient. Likewise, it can impact the decision to treat a fracture without surgery versus with surgery. If the child has more growth remaining, we trend toward avoiding surgery if possible. If we need to get more specific about predicting growth, there are systems that have been devised. There is a system for predicting progression or worsening of scoliosis in adolescents that takes into account the growth plates in the bones of the hand. All this being said, however, you should never go to an orthopedist just to see if your child is still growing or if we can predict their final height. The answer is no.

As an aside, there is also a structure called an apophysis. This is a growth plate that exists where a tendon from a muscle attaches to a bone. They do not help the bones grow longer but do allow them to grow wider. They can become irritated in children and adolescents at different ages from overuse. Heel pain in a 10-year-old is usually overuse of the apophysis on the heel bone, and we call this *Sever's Disease*. More commonly, adolescents that participate in a lot of jumping sports can suffer from activity-related knee pain where the patellar tendon (kneecap) attaches to the tibia (the shin bone). That bump on the front of your tibia is called the tibial tuberosity, and there is an apophysis located at that spot in adolescents. Overuse injury to this area is called *Osgood Schlatter's Disease*. Thankfully, none of these conditions close the growth plate or affect development, but they can be persistently painful until the growth plates close from normal completion of bone growth.

Summary time: bones develop from a cartilage precursor model that gets turned into bone as you grow, growth plates are the major sites of bone growth, usually at the ends of the bones, and bones are hard, but can change in response to different alterations in their environments, unlike manmade structures. You got it? And now you know a basic version of how bones work!

Chapter 3

Learning from Injuries

Now that you have an understanding of the basics, we will address a good way to view injuries to bones in children, including examples. Many readers are curious as to what makes a doctor nervous with respect to childhood injuries. I see and treat many children's injuries on a daily basis. I have also helped treat many more severe injuries during my residency training when I worked at a level one trauma center (where all the horrible stuff goes). The rest of this chapter will be devoted to explaining my worldview on children's healing potential.

As a reminder, the overall goal of this book is to move toward redirecting parental anxiety toward the few specific things that really matter so that the rest of the day can be a little more relaxed. Parenting carries enough anxiety on its own, and it's best to keep things in perspective. This is not *1000 Ways for Your Child to Die* (which is what my poor wife seems to live regularly in her head). This is *There are a Few Things That Really Could Permanently Injure or Kill Your Children and The Rest Isn't as Big of a Deal as You Might Be Worried About*. My job is to empower you as a parent to remain levelheaded in stressful situations and feel confident in caring for your kids.

Let's see what children's injuries look like from a limb and body perspective. Children's injuries are remarkably common, and children heal remarkably well. They are literally made to heal. I will explain here what does NOT make me nervous as an orthopedist, and in a subsequent chapter we will get to what some of you really want to know: What *does* make an orthopedist get nervous about children?

The Term "Fracture"

What does an orthopedist mean when they say "fracture"? I think most people tend to think of a fracture as a small crack in the bone whereas a "broken" bone is one that is either broken all the way through (what we call a displaced fracture). The term *fracture* means a rupture in the bone structure. For orthopedists, the word *fracture* includes all types of breaks in the bone and there is no distinction between a "broken bone" and a *fracture*; they are one and the same. There are many adjectives we use with the word *fracture* to describe the pattern of the fracture, but I think the terms most people should know are "nondisplaced" and "displaced." A *nondisplaced* fracture is a break in the bone without a shift in the overall alignment of the bone. Think of this as a crack in the bone. A *displaced* fracture is one where the pieces have shifted out of alignment. The term *displaced* can encompass a wide range. It could be as small as a two-millimeter shift in alignment, or it could be where the two bone ends are splintered into pieces and aren't even touching anymore. Despite verbal descriptions of fractures, we orthopedists love pictures. Pictures really are worth a thousand words in our line of work.

The Resiliency of Children

God made children to be incredibly resilient to injury because he knew how clumsy children would be. That's what I believe. I tell this to patients all the time when dealing with fracture care. Because children are so prone to injury, they are also prone to healing very well. Children have incredible regenerative potential. In modern times, certain injury patterns to the limb are more common in children than they are in adults, partly due to the differences in activities (not many adults are routinely climbing monkey bars or jumping from swing sets) but mostly due to the nature of children's bones.

One of the best teachers in life is experience. When I was early in my second year of residency, my oldest son fell down a set of stairs when he was about 18 months old. We were staying at a mountain cabin with a lot of extended family members. There were many small children around, and there was a set of stairs located on the front porch that descended approximately 15 feet total. The stairs themselves were very tall, not like a standard stairway in a house. They were old and wooden. My wife and I had discussed the stairway the second we arrived, and we were going to be extra cautious about it because our son was at a dangerous walking stage, and he could move fairly quickly. However, one time I let my son out and turned to hold the door open for another child to come out, and when I turned back around, my son was at the top of the stairs. I could see it happening in slow motion before it happened. He fell down those stairs almost like a slinky and hit the bottom hard on a paved driveway. I chased him down as fast as I could, and my heart dropped. I had failed my son and thought he wasn't moving his legs for a second. I panicked and raced him to the ER with my wife as fast as possible. Of course, I was scared, and my wife was hysterical. After a quick discussion with the ER physician, no head scan was needed. He was moving everything and had not lost consciousness. We were discharged shortly thereafter. My son was extra fussy for that night and had a large bruise on his head, but by the next evening he was acting essentially normal. It then hit me how remarkable children are at both resisting severe injury and healing from injury, but also how every parent can make a mistake. It showed me that God knew children were going to get hurt and that He made them very tough. As one emergency medicine physician told one of my best friends in a similar situation, "babies bounce." However, I have no regret in taking him to the ER that day, and you should always err on the side of caution when in doubt.

For some, the God answer may not satisfy, so let's take a minute to discuss natural selection and evolutionary biology principles. As a quick refresher, the concept of natural selection essentially explains why life has developed the way that it has across all organisms. Animals, for instance, are well suited to their environments because of the "survival of the fittest." If a genetic change results in the development of a survival advantage in a certain animal in a certain circumstance, nature will selectively push for the survival of that advantage through subsequent generations. For instance, if a taller neck or a longer tongue in a mammal population leads to better survival because of better ability to reach food on taller trees with longer thorns, then you might end up with an animal like a giraffe, which is well suited to its environment. In other words, nature selects for these advantages.

The other important concept of evolutionary biology is the definition of the purpose of life. From the standpoint of evolutionary biology, the only true purpose in life is to survive long enough to reproduce, and then for your offspring to be able to reproduce. There are all sorts of nuances to how different organisms accomplish this, but in the case of *Homo sapiens* (humans), we need to survive to reproductive age and then ensure the survival of our offspring long enough for them to be able to reproduce as well, thus ensuring the survival of our lineage. For humans, the age of reproduction would be the onset of sexual maturation, which includes ability for males to produce sperm and females to begin menstrual cycles as opportunities for egg fertilization. This is, of course, accompanied by the *desire* to reproduce as well (Damn those pesky adolescent hormones!)

Whether or not a 16-year-old is capable of raising a child in the modern era is irrelevant to evolutionary biology. There was no such concern from the genetic standpoint in prior ages. You needed to live long enough to get through puberty, then produce as many children as you could and try to keep them alive. Of course, at that time the rates of death were *significantly* higher than they are now. It was not uncommon even up to 100 years ago to lose one or multiple children, usually before the age of 1. It was also incredibly risky as a woman to have a child due to the risk of dying from the act of childbirth itself. Let us take a moment to recognize how incredible modern medicine is. We should also recognize that there are many people on the globe who do not have as much access to it as we do in the United States.

As an aside, one explanation for menopause in women around the average age of 51 is that menopause might be considered an evolutionary advantage in terms of being a grandmother. The idea is that you would do better to NOT be pregnant at age 55 (I'm sure many women would agree!) in order to ensure the survival of your genes. You might be better served assisting in the care of your grandchildren, who are your genetic offspring, rather than trying to survive birthing a child at that age (Can you imagine?). Perhaps nature selected this as an advantage because early humans did better when the older generations helped to support the young while the parents were accomplishing other tasks or caring for the ones they had just birthed.

As another aside, generally at around age 45 to 50 is when you see the leading cause of death become cancer for adults in the United States. This makes sense from an evolutionary standpoint as well. At that point as a caveman, you would have lived long enough to produce children and keep them alive long enough to produce their own children (25 years for yourself, 25 years for your children). At that point, if mechanisms in the body started breaking down and illnesses of the body became more common, there is not nearly as much of a survival advantage for you to be able to robustly resist those tendencies because you have already served your purpose.

(Unfortunately, evolutionary biology doesn't see a relaxing retirement on the beach near a golf course as a life goal. If it did, many of us physicians wouldn't have a job.) Of course, many would die well before the age of 50 as well from various illnesses, but the point remains: for the majority of our existence as humans, life expectancy was not nearly as high as it is today.

I've rambled on for a bit, but here's why: from a natural selection standpoint, children who were more resistant to injury definitely survive better than their peers. For this reason, children should predictably survive certain types of injuries, heal well, and become successful adults. If falling from ground height and breaking your arm at the age of 5 led to you to lose complete or significant function of the arm, many aspects of life would become much more difficult, especially prior to the past century. Yet millions of children have broken their limbs for thousands of years and did not suffer any prolonged disability, though there can always be exceptions. Also keep in mind that humanity has existed for much longer than the past 70 years. We were designed for a period without modern medical advancements, and much of our history has progressed without these advancements available.

Now we can discuss what I call "caveman medicine." Given my prior discussion on the survival of humanity prior to modern medical advancements, I will define *Caveman Medicine* as taking advantage of the natural healing ability of the human body to direct our own modern medical treatment. With *Caveman Medicine,* I view it as injuries that cavepeople would have suffered from normal activities thousands of years ago, such as falling from a low tree branch or falling from a ground height. Rest assured, if your child comes into my office, I will not treat him or her like a caveperson although I'm sure you might occasionally think your child is one. I will also not speak to them in grunts although many other physician colleagues think that this is all we orthopedists are capable of. This is one of those "don't lose the forest through trees" ideas. Children are made to survive being broken. Approximately 42% of boys and 27% of girls will sustain a broken bone prior to the age of 16.[1] They are miraculous healers and can mend injuries much better than adults can. In general, the younger the patient, the more regenerative potential, and the quicker and better they will heal. I will give some specific examples.

Upper Arm Fractures

Proximal humerus fractures are fractures that occur in the upper portion of the humerus bone, which is the part of the arm where the biceps and triceps muscles reside.

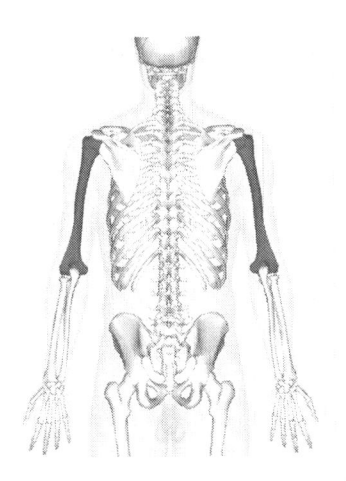

Image credit Anatomography under the license Creative Commons Attribution-Share Alike 2.1 Japan, Image link: https://commons.wikimedia.org/wiki/File:Humerus_-_posterior_view.pngWikimedia Commons, license link: https://creativecommons.org/licenses/by-sa/2.1/jp/deed.en

The top part of the humerus is part of the shoulder joint. Fractures in this area are not very common fractures for children and account for less than 5% of fractures in children with open growth plates. These fractures usually occur at a growth plate in the portion of the humerus that is near the shoulder joint, where the humerus meets the shoulder blade. As a general rule, the closer you break a bone to a growth plate, and the more remaining growth that plate has, the less you need to worry about the bone being significantly displaced, or in layman's terms, horribly crooked.

Through good observational research, we keep track of "acceptable deformities" for different fracture patterns in both adults and children. For the term *acceptable deformities*, think of it as "how crooked can the bone be before the orthopedist has to intervene." This includes shortening of bone fragments, new abnormal angles to the bone, overlapping of bone ends, and rotation of the broken bone among others. *Observational research* in this case means reviewing documented outcomes of the many ways fractures have been treated in the past. This includes the initial deformity and the eventual final outcome in the child's limb. The acceptable deformity for a *proximal humerus fracture* in a child under the age of ten is three letters: a-n-y. That's right, "any." It does not matter how displaced or terrible the X-ray might look. It will heal and straighten well. Even the acceptable deformity from ages 10-12 seems extreme, with some studies suggesting up to 75 degrees of an angle being acceptable because the arm will straighten with time. Think about that as healing potential!

Clavicle, or collarbone, fractures occur somewhat frequently during birth, with an estimated range from 0.2 to 3.5% of all vaginal deliveries.[2]

Clavicle fracture

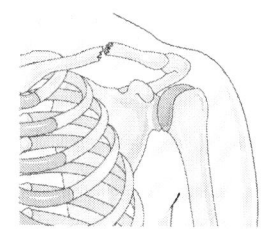

Image credit Laboratoires Servier SMART-Servier Medical Cart under the license Creative Commons Attribution-Share Alike 3.0 Unported, Image link: https://commons.wikimedia.org/wiki/File: Collarbone_fracture_-_Clavicle_fracture_--_Smart-Servier.jpg, license link: https://creativecommons.org/licenses/by-sa/3.0/

The number is even higher for breech deliveries, which rarely happen nowadays due to better safety and the use of Cesarean sections. However, not so long ago, C-sections were not an option for birth. Or at least they were less commonly utilized prior to surgical safety advancements, and it is likely that the number of shoulder fractures from births were previously even higher than they are now in the era of modern medicine. So how do we treat these fractures? We might put a sling or wrap on the infant's shoulder to provide some comfort, but in reality, you probably don't need to do anything. They heal, and they heal quickly. They do not typically cause any long-term dysfunction to the limb on their own.

I have treated these fractures on occasion after a particularly vigorous birth trauma, usually because of an emergency called *shoulder dystocia* in which the shoulder is trapped and cannot be easily delivered despite the head being in the canal.

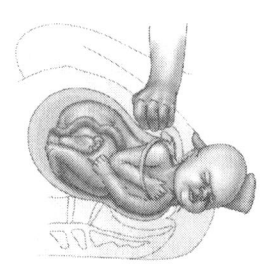

Image credit Henry Lerner under the license Creative Commons Attribution-Share Alike 4.0 International, Image link: https:// commons.wikimedia.org/wiki/File:Suprapubic-pressureforSD.jpg , license link: https://creativecommons.org/licenses/by/4.0/

This places great risk to both the mother and the child. Sometimes in order to deliver the child successfully, an obstetrician may have to be more aggressive with certain maneuvers. Occasionally an obstetrician may even have to purposefully break the clavicle. Fortunately, this is rare, and it is not the fault of the obstetrician. They are trying to safely deliver a child, and life matters more than trying to prevent limb injury.

I should mention a different medical condition that can occur during the birthing process called *Obstetric Brachial Plexopathy*. In this disorder, you get a stretch to the nerves in the shoulder, which is different than a simple fracture to the clavicle. This injury can cause certain arm muscles to either not work or be very weak. Again, I want to emphasize that this is a rare condition and is not the fault of negligence by the medical staff or the mother. Even with severe injury to the nerves, 90% of these completely resolve because of the remarkable ability of children, especially infants, to heal. The same injury to adults could cause permanent disability to the arm. It makes sense that babies can heal the above injuries well, because if they couldn't, survival to adulthood would be very difficult because cavemen didn't have many options.

Buckle and Toddler's Fractures

Moving from birth to childhood, *Buckle Fractures* are incomplete fractures that only occur in children.

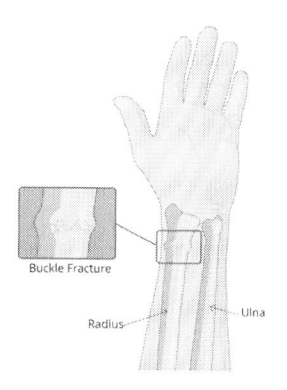

Image credit RouDhi under the license Creative Commons Attribution-Share Alike 4.0 International, Image link: https://commons.wikimedia.org/wiki/File:Buckle_fracture_of_the_Radius.svg , license link: https://creativecommons.org/licenses/by/4.0/

They are fractures in which the bone bends rather than breaks all the way through. Children's bones are soft enough to undergo this injury pattern, whereas adults' bones are not. Our bones are too brittle. These fractures most commonly occur near the wrist and can easily be treated with a removable brace if the child is agreeable. I usually give parents the choice if they want a fiberglass cast or a removable brace. The biggest advantage of the brace is being able to take it off to bathe or let it dry off if it accidentally gets wet. I trust the child's parent to tell me what they think is best for their child. A lot of mothers with young boys look at me as if I were crazy to even suggest a removable brace and immediately request the cast. The cast or brace is really just acting as a protective shell to prevent further injury.

Another example of children being "made to break" is the *Toddler's Fracture*, which is a fracture of the tibia (i.e. shin bone) in a child around age 2 to 3. It usually happens because of a twist while wrestling a brother or a fall, and sometimes the injury may not be witnessed by an adult. The child will either refuse to walk or will limp instead. Usually, we obtain an x-ray if suspicious, and occasionally we will not actually see the fracture if it is nondisplaced, or the so-called "hairline fracture." Casting the leg for three weeks usually does the trick.

Between *Buckle Fractures* and *Toddler's Fractures*, these are the ultimate *Caveman Medicine* topics to me. We treat them because of modern medicine, and we can certainly help to decrease pain and chances of further injury. The reality is many children sustained these injuries prior to modern medicine, and they did fine and did not have permanent disability. X-rays were not discovered until 1895, and they were not widely used for medical diagnostics for many decades after. For that matter, antibiotics were not even around one hundred years ago, and their discovery has had one of the largest impacts on world health.

Prior to wide availability of X-ray machines, *Buckle Fractures* and *Toddler's Fractures* still occurred in high numbers, just as high as today. But what usually happened is that a child would limp or refuse to use the limb for a few days or even a week or two. The child would eventually heal and start using the limb again, even without an intervention. (As an aside, the history of medicine really is fascinating. Prior to X-rays, the only way of diagnosing fractures was to cut someone open while either living or dead and look directly at the bone because there was no other way to see inside the body. For a long time, there were even debates on what the exact reason was for limbs becoming deformed after an injury. Most thought it was a dislocation rather than a break, and it was difficult for physicians to treat these appropriately for a long period of time because they did not even know exactly what they were treating.)

Forearm Fractures

Another common entity is the *Both Bone Forearm Fracture*. No fancy name for this one. We orthopedists aren't as clever as our colleagues to change the name to Latin or come up with a more creative name. It literally is what it says it is: when you break both bones in your forearm, the radius and the ulna.

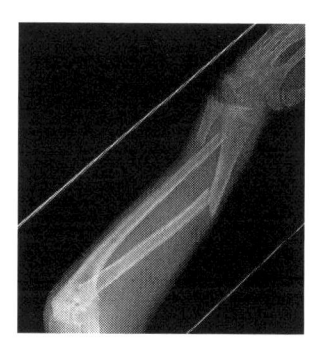

Image credit James Heilman, MD under the license Creative Commons Attribution-Share Alike 4.0 International, Image link: https://commons.wikimedia.org/wiki/File:FracRadUlna.png, license link: https://creativecommons.org/licenses/by/4.0/

Treating these injuries is often a rewarding experience on my end, but the injury itself can be very traumatic for the patient and their parents. My nephew had one of these recently and had to be in a cast most of the summer, a true torture for him and his parents. This usually occurs from a ground level fall in children ages 4 to 14 and is estimated to be around 40% of all pediatric fractures, if you include the wrist.[3] *Both Bone Fractures* peak around age 13-14 in males and 11-12 in females. At age 13, males are twice as likely to sustain these fractures as their female counterparts. They are the most common fracture associated with backyard trampoline use and the second most common associated with falls from monkey bars.[1] I have also seen this injury commonly from football or other sports where children fall to the ground violently.

This one usually terrifies parents because the forearm can look very crooked. Typically, we must sedate the child and correct the deformity with good ole fashion elbow grease. Nothing is a more "caveman treatment" than to take a crooked forearm and make it straight. Though it's often more technical than just pushing the bone back into place, our non-orthopedic colleagues probably think we have a textbook chapter that describes these maneuvers as "Arm no look straight. Me fix bone now. To fix bone is simple: just make arm not look crooked no more, grunt." Once we get the arm into a more favorable position, we allow the bone to heal on its own by placing it into a cast or splint, taking advantage of the body's natural ability. We then rely on the child's remaining growth to straighten out any remaining small deformities. However, if an adolescent is nearing the end of growth, this may push us toward a surgical treatment.

Considering the acceptable deformity range for *Both Bone Forearm Fractures*, younger children tolerate worse deformities or angles because of their remaining growth potential and remodeling potential. From ages 0 to 10, you can accept an angle of up to 15 degrees. However, at age 10 and above you must be 10 degrees or less. If you are within 2 years of skeletal maturity, i.e. completion of bone growth, you cannot tolerate any angulation or rotation of the fracture, it needs to essentially be perfect. Again, *Both Bone Forearm Fractures* are common now, and they were common 500 years ago. Though having the arm alignment improved and casted is absolutely a better treatment than what was available in prior centuries, the forearm still has remarkable growth potential to correct bad deformities from an injury, or at least the point where it did not impact the overall function of the limb.

I will take a moment to compare treating *Both Bone Forearm Fractures* in children to treating adults because it illustrates a point. *Both Bone Forearm Fractures* are less common in adults and usually this type of fracture takes a more severe trauma, such as a car wreck, to befall an adult. Adults have essentially no remodeling potential, at least to "grow out of" a deformity. Natural healing processes still occur, just not as quickly as children. If you let the fracture ends stay displaced, they will heal in that poor position or even fail to heal altogether, and the forearm will have significant trouble providing you rotation in the wrist. Therefore, we perform surgery to line the bones up in their anatomical positions and plate them with screws as an internal brace to hold them in position. The bone then heals across the fracture sites while the patient is still able to move their wrist and forearm. We recommend surgery even for nondisplaced fractures. Casts in children generally must go above the elbow for a long period during the healing process for *Both Bone* fractures. If you were to cast an adult, the elbow and wrist would become extremely stiff. Historically, this was known as *Cast Disease*, which was a result of immobilizing someone for too long. Adults just do not have the same healing capacity as children. Therefore, we perform surgery in adults to avoid casting in addition to the other healing advantages. The same fractures in an adult require significantly different treatment than those in children. I've discussed just a small smattering of injury patterns, but the important thing to take away is how well children heal.

Jordan Paynter, MD

Fractures Often Treated with Surgery

Though I've discussed many fractures we treat without surgery, sometimes limb injuries heal better with surgery, so what's the distinction? Many of the child limb injuries we treat with surgery are done so because of various treatments tried in the past with research on the results. This field is always evolving, but in general children need surgery way less often than adults, especially in younger children. Many fractures that require surgery for the best outcomes are because of inappropriate alignment or a fracture near or inside of a joint. Typically, the farther you are away from a joint, the better your limb can tolerate being misaligned.

The most common childhood fracture treated with surgery is the *Supracondylar Humerus Fracture*, which occurs in the elbow. They are the most common elbow fractures in children and are most common in children ages 5 to 6.[1] *Supracondylar Fractures* usually happen after a fall onto an outstretched hand and are the most common fracture associated with monkey bars.[1] Not all of them require surgery, only the ones that are displaced.

Gartland classification

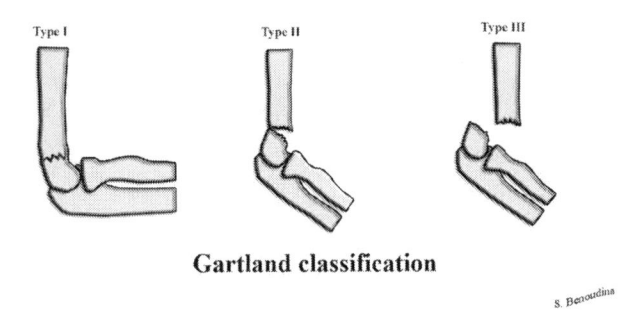

Image credit Benoudina samir under the license Creative Commons Attribution-Share Alike 4.0 International, Image link: https://commons.wikimedia.org/wiki/File: Gartland_Classification.jpg , license link: https:// creativecommons.org/licenses/by/4.0/

In most cases, the child is put to sleep and the bone is realigned and pinned into place with metal wires. The arm is then casted for 3-4 weeks, and the pins are removed around that time. Research has shown us that certain fracture patterns heal better with surgery for both functional outcomes and lower likelihood of subsequent injuries. Occasionally, a child will have a severely displaced fracture that is functionally acting as an elbow dislocation and is putting pressure on the arteries and nerves of the elbow. These are treated more urgently and have more potential serious consequences if ignored.

Most of the time fractures near the wrist are treated successfully with manipulation and casting, but occasionally a piece of the periosteum (soft tissue layer that surrounds the bone) can become entrapped between the bone fragments in extreme cases. No matter how hard you try to manipulate the wrist, the bone simply will not line up. In these cases, surgery is usually necessary to remove the entrapped flap of tissue so the bone can be realigned appropriately. We may place a pin across the fracture site to hold it in place before we cast the child. The pin is removed a few weeks later in the office.

Severe Injuries

Let's say your child does end up with a terrible injury. I have, so far, mentioned common injuries that children can heal. What if they sustain an injury that they cannot heal? Well, even the adaptability of children is remarkable compared to that of adults. They have more brain cells than we do and can rewire those cells in incredible ways. If you have ever observed someone who lost a limb at a young age, say less than 10, versus someone who lost a limb at age 50, you know what I'm talking about. Children can grow to function almost normally, or at least adapt to their deformity fairly well. There is a woman by the internet name of Tisha UnArmed who has a channel on YouTube who was born without arms. She has many videos documenting how she does life with only her two legs and feet. It is incredible to watch, and on my own observation, her feet seem to have adapted handlike qualities. Her big toes curl inward like thumbs and her foot shape is broader. Essentially, she adapted from a birth defect to function very well on her own. She can drive a modified vehicle and pump gas at a regular filling station, and she has videos of some of her daily activities. If you did the same to an adult who had lived their whole life with two arms, they would have a miserable time with it and would not survive without significant help.

Likewise, nerve repairs and replanting limbs and fingers in children is significantly more successful than in adults. One of the biggest reasons for this is the superior ability of children to heal nerve damage because they are young and have more stem cells available. Whenever we perform nerve repairs, the biggest predictor of recovery and return of function is age: the younger the better. When limbs are accidentally amputated, children recover better for the same reason when replanted. FYI, not every limb can be replanted depending on the type and level of injury. Sometimes we have no option for replantation. As for finger replantation, again the recovery is significantly better in children. There are certain situations for replanting fingers in children that we would not attempt in adults due to the better healing potential of children, whereas it would be a fool's tasks to attempt in an adult because of the certainty of failure.

I have seen multiple causes of nerve injuries and amputations during training. I've seen children get their fingers amputated by sticking their hand into a running lawn mower blade, having their fingers run over by ice skates, and animal bites to name a few. I've even seen an arm torn off a child from an industrial dryer when trying to retrieve their blanket prior to the spin cycle ending. I've seen nerve injuries from deep wounds from knives or broken glass and even an accidental gunshot from a handgun into the forearm by an older brother. I do not treat these injuries in my practice, but I have witnessed the results of the healing capabilities of children through these experiences, though they don't always heal perfectly. I've seen similar injuries in adults, and there is a dramatic difference in how well the children do compared with adults.

There's a fascinating surgery called a *Van Ness Rotationplasty* that only works because of the ability of a child's brain to remodel. It is a rare procedure done for cancer in the region of the knee or for children with certain limb deformities. You remove the bottom half of the femur (thigh bone) and the top part of the tibia (shin bone) and leave the soft tissue in between. You then shorten the remaining leg and flip the foot and ankle completely backward, 180 degrees, and connect the remaining femur to the remaining tibia. The ankle then becomes a sort of functional knee and allows the child to use a below knee prosthesis (false leg) rather than an above knee amputation prosthesis. Below knee amputations are a lot easier on the body functionally than above knee amputations. The backward foot acts as an attachment point for the prosthesis. There is a TikTok personality named Emily Fogle who has one, and I recommend you check out her page if you're interested in what this looks like (Emily Fogle (@emilylfogle) | TikTok). You also keep the growth plates, so the child's limb can continue to grow. This is limited to children under the age of ten. It is worth an internet search on some people who have undergone this procedure. It looks bizarre but functions incredibly well, and it is only possible because of the ability of a child to relearn how to move and remodel their brain accordingly. You absolutely could not do this to an adult and have the same result.

Common Fracture Tidbits

For the sake of education, I would be remiss if I didn't include a segment with some common factoids on fractures in children and adolescents. Upper extremity fractures are more common than lower extremity fractures. The radius (forearm bone that includes the widest portion of the wrist) is the most commonly broken bone, and males are 2-3 times more likely to have these injuries compared to females.[4] The humerus (upper arm bone) is the second most commonly broken bone.[1] Fracture incidence in girls peaks around age 12, just before adolescence. In boys, fracture incidence peaks around age 14-15.[5]

Boys are more likely to sustain fractures than girls, with a ratio of 2.7 to 1 overall.[1] Some of this can be explained by increased participation in sports activities, but some of it has behavioral explanations. One study reviewed street crossings per day and compared the incidence of boys versus girls being hit by a car between ages 5-8. Though the number of street crossings were similar between the two genders, boys were more often injured.[1] We boys are more likely to engage in riskier behaviors, so good luck to all you parents with boys! Thank goodness I only have three of them.

Interestingly, the left arm is more commonly injured than the right arm with a ratio of 1.3 to 1 according to *Rockwood and Wilkin's Fractures in Children*, which is our orthopedic go-to textbook for fracture care.[1] This is thought to be due to the fact that most people are right hand dominant and are using their right hand for the activity at the time of injury. The left arm is used for protection more commonly because it is free.

Not surprisingly, children tend to sustain more fractures during the warmer months of the year which correlates with both more reasons to be outside and play as well as summer vacation, providing support for the old adage "idle hands are the devil's workshop." The more free time children have, the more likely they are to be injured. Interestingly, in some studies there are peaks in December despite it being a colder month, likely due to Christmas breaks and new toys. On a daily basis, children are more often injured in the afternoon, with one study showing a peak around 6 pm.[1]

Learning by Real Life Experience

I would like to give another example of a child's healing ability. Recently, my oldest son was jumping on a trampoline (I know, what kind of orthopedic surgeon would own a trampoline?) and some doofus broke his foot. It was the first broken bone in our family. Who was the doofus who injured him? That would be me. You can only imagine the grief I caught for this from my wife. My son loves it when I bounce with him (which you shouldn't do according to experts!), and one time I bounced him too high. The extra force of him landing with his foot and toes pointed down put a lot of energy through the arch of his foot. He broke the third metatarsal. The metatarsals are the bones that make up the forward part of the arch of your foot.

Image credit BodyParts 3D by Database Center for Life Science under the license Creative Commons Attribution-Share Alike 2.1 Japan, Image link: https://commons.wikimedia.org/wiki/File: Metatarsal_bones01_-_superior_view.png , license link: https:// creativecommons.org/licenses/by-sa/2.1/jp/

I knew I had done something wrong by the way he started crying severely and was unable to walk. We took him into my office and got an x-ray. I placed him into a removable Velcro boot and gave him some crutches. The next day, we walked him into school (a walk of shame for me of course), and he used his crutches. Two days later, he had ditched the crutches and was fine in the boot. After about three weeks, he had no pain and was back into his normal shoe. Despite a broken bone in the foot, he was able to rebound quickly.

In this chapter, we have discussed the ability of children to heal through a look at the orthopedic world. Of course, there are many other injury patterns that we could discuss, and I do not want to belittle injury, just to show how children are made to heal and overcome disability. God made them resilient because He knew they were going to get hurt and get hurt often. My point with the chapter was to illustrate this concept and hopefully give you a little bit of reassurance that children's injuries will heal the vast majority of time without permanent disability, even in cases that require surgery. I did not discuss surgical injuries here, but sometimes even children need surgery for fracture treatment. Remember, the point of this book is to help you take a Birdseye view of medical care and to redirect your focus on things that can truly harm your child permanently.

So, what does *not* make an orthopedist nervous with his own children? Limb injuries from ground level falls. I even own a trampoline, but I regularly check it for tears or damage, and it has a net. We have a playground, and we try to be cautious, but I am not as worried about serious injury or death arising from such objects as long as reasonable caution is taken. I will cover this in a subsequent chapter. In the next chapter, we will discuss what actually kills children in the 21st century and then discuss ways to avoid it in subsequent chapters. My goal is to help you focus your attention on the things that can actually kill your child to help put your mind at ease so you can reduce your anxiety about the physical harm that can befall your child. We will also discuss the activities and injury patterns that can severely injure your child and potentially cause permanent disability.

Lastly, as a disclaimer: although the injuries discussed in this chapter may not cause severe or permanent disability or death, you should still seek appropriate medical evaluation and treatment when they are suspected. I also recognize that severe injuries can and do occur to some children, sometimes resulting in permanent disability and even death. Fortunately, these are uncommon, but we will address these in subsequent chapters.

* * *

References

1. David Skaggs MD, John Flynn MD, Peter Waters MD. *Rockwood and Wilkins' Fractures in Children*. 8th ed. Wolters Kluwer Health; 2015:1288.

2. Kaplan B, Rabinerson D, Avrech OM, Carmi N, Steinberg DM, Merlob P. Fracture of the clavicle in the newborn following normal labor and delivery. *Int J Gynaecol Obstet*. Oct 1998;63(1):15-20. doi:10.1016/s0020-7292(98)00127-1

3. John Edgington MD, Michael Glotzbecker MD. Both Bone Forearm Fracture - Pediatric. Updated May 19, 2024. Accessed August 6, 2024. https://www.orthobullets.com/pediatrics/4126/both-bone-forearm-fracture--pediatric?section=bullets

4. Rameez Qudsi MD, Chris Souder MD. Distal Radius Fractures - Pediatric. Updated March 3, 2024. Accessed August 6, 2024, 2024. https://www.orthobullets.com/pediatrics/4014/distal-radius-fractures--pediatric

5. Landin LA. Epidemiology of children's fractures. *J Pediatr Orthop B*. Apr 1997;6(2):79-83. doi:10.1097/01202412-199704000-00002

Chapter 4

Death Statistics

This is the chapter that many of you are probably most curious about. So far, we have discussed bumps, bruises, and broken bones, but what will actually kill your child? Likewise, knowing what I know as a physician, and specifically orthopedic surgeon, what makes me nervous about my own children's health? First, I will show statistics on the most common causes of death in children by age group, and in subsequent chapters I will break this down into prevention tips for each risk category. The goal of this is to appropriately direct your attention to true dangers for children. In the grand scheme of things, keeping your child alive is the task that ultimately matters for your child's health. There are plenty of traumatic events they can survive without much of an issue. There are just a few things that really put them in jeopardy.

Let's start out with a few lists, broken down by age. This data has been pulled from the Center for Disease Control (CDC) webpage. The CDC serves in the interest of public health and has many functions, and one major function is to track data on causes of major injury and death in the U.S. There is a section called the Web-based Injury Statistics Query and Reporting System (WISQARS) that displays recorded data collected on injuries. I have adapted the WISQARS data to create simplified lists showing the top 10 causes of death for children by age group from 2001 to 2020.[1] The lists below are for simplification and show the top 10 causes of death in children by age group. The age categories span 5 years with the exception of *under age one* and *ages 1-4*. These ages are typically separated out for review based on age-related differences in child development.

Age <1

1. Congenital Anomalies (birth defects)
2. Short gestation (born too early)
3. Sudden Infant Death Syndrome (SIDS)
4. Maternal Pregnancy Complications
5. Unintentional Injury (accidental traumas, drowning, burns, firearms, among others)
6. Placenta/Cord/Membranes (essentially suffocation during birth)
7. Bacterial Sepsis (overwhelming infection)
8. Respiratory Distress (lung issues/issues with breathing)
9. Circulatory System Disease (heart issues)
10. Neonatal Hemorrhage (excessive bleeding in newborns)

Ages 1-4

1. Unintentional Injury
2. Congenital Anomalies
3. Homicide
4. Malignant Neoplasms (cancer)
5. Heart disease
6. Influenza and pneumonia
7. Cerebrovascular (pediatric stroke)

8. Perinatal period (children with terminal birth defects or traumas that live past the age of 1 but subsequently expire)
9. Septicemia (overwhelming infection)
10. Benign neoplasms (non-cancerous tumors)

Ages 5-9

1. Unintentional Injury
2. Malignant Neoplasms (cancer)
3. Congenital Anomalies
4. Homicide
5. Heart Disease
6. Chronic Lower Respiratory Disease (usually includes diseases like Cystic Fibrosis)
7. Influenza and Pneumonia
8. Cerebrovascular (pediatric stroke)
9. Benign Neoplasms (non-cancerous tumors)
10. Septicemia (overwhelming infection)

Ages 10-14

1. Unintentional Injury
2. Malignant Neoplasms (cancer)
3. Suicide
4. Homicide
5. Congenital Anomalies
6. Heart Disease
7. Chronic Lower Respiratory Disease
8. Influenza and Pneumonia
9. Cerebrovascular (pediatric stroke)
10. Benign Neoplasms (non-cancerous tumors)

Ages 15-19

1. Unintentional Injury
2. Homicide
3. Suicide
4. Malignant Neoplasms (cancer)
5. Heart Disease
6. Congenital Anomalies
7. Influenza and Pneumonia
8. Chronic Lower Respiratory Disease
9. Cerebrovascular (pediatric stroke)
10. Diabetes Mellitus

That is a lot of data to chew through. Let's break this down. Notice that *all* of the age groups with the exception of infants (children less than age 1) have unintentional injury as the leading cause of death. Unfortunately, this category encompasses multiple different causes of death, but we can alternatively call these "accidental trauma," which includes car wrecks, drowning, etc. Notice also that suicide creeps onto the list in older children. The category *Homicide* does not usually mean pre-meditated murder in younger children but rather a "non-accidental trauma" or child abuse.

There are a lot of categories that sound terrible, and of course they are, but I would like us to all take a step back from these lists and breathe for a minute. I am writing this book assuming your child does not have major medical issues, such as a severe genetic abnormality or heart condition. These are awful conditions, but most parents know either before birth or shortly afterward if their child suffers from these conditions and will likely be aware that their child's battle with the serious condition is the overriding concern. Fortunately, these are not terribly common. I would also like to point out that children with some of these serious conditions also end up being more susceptible to things like the flu and overwhelming infection in the body because they usually do not have normal functioning immune systems, so sometimes this can inflate the statistics on *influenza* or *septicemia*.

My goal with this information is *not* to scare but to educate, reduce overall stress, and potentially save a life. So, let's further break this down into the things we *can* control as parents and the things we usually *cannot* control. The presence of heart disease, cancer, birth defects, etc. are not circumstances that we can control. For simplicity's sake, we are going to address data from the year 2019 going forward. As of writing this in 2024, data is readily available through 2021, but 2019 makes the most sense to analyze because it was the year before the Covid-19 pandemic started. It was the last full year before Covid potentially skewed numbers because more children were out of school, fewer people were traveling, and perhaps the rates of other diseases went down due to less transmission from social distancing. We are likely trending toward normalcy over the past year or two, but data on 2022 and 2023 are not readily available at the time I am writing. The year 2019 is the closest year that would represent what I would call a "normal risk year" for the modern age. If *Bare Bones* gains popularity, I will release updated versions with newer numbers every three to five years.

Speaking of Covid-19, we know that it has been on full blast from the media for the past few years, and there are good reasons for that. We certainly achieved a heightened sense of germ theory and washing our hands from the experiences of the past few years. How many children actually died from Covid-19? As of July 28, 2023, over the first three years of the pandemic, 776 children ages 0-4 and 1,071 ages 5-18 died from Covid-19. In 2021, there were 73.6 million total living children between the ages of 0-18.[2] If you do the math, that is a rate of 0.000008% deaths per year from Covid in children ages 0-18, or less than 1 in 100,000. I don't point this out to belittle Covid-19 and its impact, but to point out how aware of the situation we were during the worst parts of the pandemic. Yet we forget to keep our attention focused on things that are more commonly harmful to our children, such as drowning or choking, which carry higher death rates.

Let me also take a minute to discuss one of the potentially terrifying things that every parent fears for their child: cancer. My heart goes out to any parent who has walked through a cancer journey with their child. Cancer is a horrible condition, but many who are diagnosed with cancer under the age of 14 survive, with a recent statistic of 85% of those diagnosed living more than 5 years after diagnosis.[3] Living beyond 5 years from diagnosis does not automatically mean the cancer has been cured, but this is typically how we measure cancer survival because it is difficult to track health data on individuals for multiple years. I want to highlight a statistic that should bring comfort: only 1,272 children aged 0-14 died from cancer out of 60,570,846 total children in the year 2019. That is 0.00002% per year, or 1 in 50,000, meaning death from cancer is extremely rare. Remember, cancer is one of the things we fear but we cannot control, so in my opinion, we as parents should redirect our concerns toward the things we *can* control.

The risks of death are grouped by age because of childhood development, and the data reflect this. Under the age of 1, most children are not walking. Under the age of 6 months, most children are not crawling. When we had our second child, it made me realize how easy infants are compared to older children (aside from the sleep part!). When our second son was 2 months old, our oldest son was three. The eldest ran around the house and yard and got into everything, and he was a danger to himself. My 2-month-old son, on the other hand, could not move from the spot we left him. His major danger was if *we* put him in an unsafe spot.

Fast forward a few years to when my oldest son was 7 and our second son was 4. My oldest son was an excellent swimmer and less likely to drown if he accidentally got into the pool. My middle son was a huge danger to himself around a pool because he was learning to swim, and he was liable to think he was safe when he was not. He is also capable of sneaking away from us and getting into a nearby pool. He could not do this at 6 months of age, but he could by age 4 since he could move around easily. My advice when taking all of this in is to try to make it make sense logically. Patterns follow the movement ability of the child and the frequency with which a child is doing certain activities.

In the next section, we are going to break things down by age and then follow with chapters on safety tips. I have broken down the categories by age and I have removed the medical causes of death (cancer, heart disease, etc.) because we cannot control these as parents. I have listed the top 5 potentially preventable causes of death in order of highest frequency. The CDC groups a lot of different accidental traumas under one category, *Unintentional Injury*, but I am going to try to subdivide where able. If you would like additional information on handling infants with illnesses or concerns about fevers in a young child, the *Moms on Call*™ series is a wonderful resource. My wife used it religiously as a reference for the first few months after each child was born. Let's break things down by age and highlight only the processes that we should be alerting ourselves to as parents to protect our children from physically related harm. Here we go!

* * *

All data referenced below have been pulled from CDC WISQARS from the year 2019. Reminder, this excludes cancer, medical complications, birth defects, etc.

Under age 1

1. SIDS (1,389 deaths)
2. Suffocation/choking (1,024 deaths)
3. Motor vehicle (72 deaths)
4. Drowning (34 deaths)
5. Poisoning (17 deaths)

SIDS

What is SIDS? It stands for *Sudden Infant Death Syndrome* and mostly occurs in infants less than 6 months of age. Technically, it is unknown exactly why these children die.[4] What *is* known is how to drastically reduce the chances of your child dying from it. Prior to birth, routine prenatal care and smoking cessation (i.e. quit smoking!) are recommended to reduce chances of SIDS. Here is a list of recommendations for after birth adapted from *UpToDate*[4]:

1. Your child should sleep on their back
2. You should not co-sleep with your child, they should sleep alone
3. Firm mattress and nothing else in the crib (no soft toys, no padding, no blankets, no cushions, etc.)
4. Do not routinely use car seats for sleep
5. Do not smoke, especially inside the house or car
6. Avoid overheating (do not sleep near a heater or direct sunlight)

Breastfeeding has also been shown to protect against SIDS. This includes breastfeeding supplemented with bottle and/or formula if needed. The more months of life you breastfeed, the better. There is some support that pacifier use may reduce the risk of SIDS as well. These recommendations are current as of 2024, but new data comes forth all the time so things may change with time.

One more point about SIDS: there is currently no strong evidence that baby monitors reduce the chances of it happening. We certainly had camera-based baby monitors so we could check on our children and see if they were crying or asleep. However, my wife and I would occasionally debate about bringing the monitors with us when we visited other places because it annoyed me to have to pack even more stuff, and I argued that it did not actually help. My wife won out in the end, and I finally gave in because I will say it's nice to be able to hear if your child is fussing without having to walk up to the door with your ear next to it.

There are baby monitors available that have a sock that you can put on their feet that will report the child's oxygen levels and breathing rate. I think these can certainly bring you a little more peace of mind, but currently no quality research-based evidence has suggested that these reduce the incidence of SIDS specifically, so this does not substitute for following evidence-based recommendations for SIDS prevention. By "quality research-based evidence," I am referring to independently performed intentionally designed studies that look at death rates over time rather than anecdotes, news stories, or testimonials given by the company that sells the product. Without research-based evidence, I cannot specifically recommend for or against purchasing these products. It also means the other previously listed SIDS prevention steps have research support and should be followed.

Suffocation and Motor Vehicles

Suffocation deaths occur most commonly from food at this age. Though some older children can certainly get into toys that can suffocate them, it is less likely with your first child if you do not have toys with choking hazards. One of the potential challenges of parenting is having multiple children at different ages. While you probably wouldn't buy a set of marbles for your 9-month-old, you might for your 6-year-old. I will do a section on choking prevention later, but one of the keys is to set yourself up for success by ensuring that your child cannot access things that are unsafe to them.

As for food choking risk, *HealthyChildren.org* has a great list of what to avoid in a simple fashion at[5]: https://www.healthychildren.org/English/health-issues/injuries-emergencies/Pages/Choking-Prevention.aspx

The CDC has a similar list with advice on how to introduce

appropriate foods at[6]: https://www.cdc.gov/nutrition/InfantandTod dlerNutrition/foods-and-drinks/choking-hazards.html

The *Motor Vehicle* category will be addressed in the next chapter with safety tips. This category includes children killed in car wrecks, being hit by a car on foot, motorcycles, all-terrain vehicles (ATVs) etc. Drowning is actually pretty darn rare for this age group. This is probably explained by the fact that infants rarely can move away from you quickly enough to get themselves into a body of water without you noticing. However, infants *can* drown and certainly *have* drowned in bathtubs, even in as little as one inch of water in some reports. My biggest advice with drowning prevention in infants is to never walk away from your child when they are in a bathtub at this age, even a small tub. The *poisoning* category includes exposure to household products as well as unintentional overdose of medication or accidentally administering a medication that is inappropriate for a child.

Ages 1-4

1. Drowning (425 deaths)
2. Homicide (311 deaths)
3. Motor vehicle (284 deaths)
4. Suffocation/choking (118 deaths)
5. Fire/burns (75 deaths)
6. Firearm - accidental (40 deaths)

As we get into the next age range, toddlers begin exploring their surroundings more as they become more mobile. However, they do not yet have spatial awareness to recognize danger. Drowning is the biggest risk for your child in this age group. This is due to a combination of the ability to move around freely and the inability to swim, sometimes added to the inability of the child's brain to process danger. Swimming pools are the biggest risk, though children drown in natural bodies of water as well, such as oceans, rivers, and lakes. Bathtubs are still not risk free either. The situations in my experience revolve around accidental neglect near a pool. We will address tips to avoid this disaster in a subsequent chapter.

Homicide at this age is often a result of child abuse and often unintentional in the sense that the perpetrator does not usually intend to cause death, but it occurs as a result of the abuse. Though there are certainly cases of premeditated murder, these are rare within this group. We will discuss risk factors in a subsequent chapter. We will also address accidental firearm deaths as well and prevention in a subsequent chapter, which is why I included it as number six.

For reference, cancer deaths would be number 3 on this list at 307 deaths, slightly behind homicide. I mentioned earlier that cancer is typically one of the biggest fears for many parents, yet ultimately drowning is routinely more deadly in children ages 1-4. Homicide and cancer are relatively close in number, and they sometimes alternate as to which one is more common depending on the year.

Ages 5-9

1. Motor vehicle (319 deaths)
2. Homicide (169 deaths)
3. Drowning (117 deaths)
4. Fire/burn (60 deaths)
5. Suffocation/choking (38 deaths)

As we get into school aged children, kids are getting involved with more activities and are less attached to caregivers. They are aware of some dangers but not all of them and can still put themselves in harm's way. Notice that the risk of drowning decreases but does not disappear. Children in this age group are still at risk of drowning. However, from age 5 until the age of 45, *Unintentional Trauma*, mostly motor vehicle crashes, is the leading cause of death even when including medical causes of death like heart disease or birth defects. After age 45, cancer takes over as the leading cause of death until age 65, when it becomes heart disease from then on. Children are still at risk for suffocation at this age, but thankfully it becomes less common as children age.

Cancer is still a leading cause of death (382 deaths) outside of the *Unintentional Injury* category. For reference, *Unintentional Injury* is the combined deaths of *motor vehicle, drowning, fires/burns,* and *suffocation* among others. When reading sources, it can sometimes be tricky depending on how the lists are grouped. It is always a good idea when reading a research article or news article to make sure you understand how they are defining the terms they are using.

Age 10-14

1. Suicide (581 deaths)
2. Motor vehicle (476 deaths)
3. Homicide (285 deaths)
4. Drowning (91 deaths)
5. Poisoning (52 deaths)

I think the most disturbing category in this age group is *Suicide*. Disclaimer, I do not yet have children in this age group. I will comment as much as I can in a subsequent chapter, but this is a very hard topic to grapple with.

It's worth noting that there is another category tied for 5th with 52 deaths labeled "Transport" which has to do with the way things are coded for medical billing and diagnostic purposes. I think this group is probably just a byproduct of the medical coding process and really belongs in addition to the motor vehicle deaths. Likewise, drowning deaths still occur in this age group, as do deaths from homicide. At this age, however, firearm accidents increase, accounting for 76.5% of the total deaths from homicide. Given the way it's recorded on the WISQARS database, it's hard to know whether these are intentional injuries or accidental discharges, but we will discuss it in a subsequent chapter.

Poisoning deaths are higher in this age group as well, though still uncommon. Alarmingly, nearly 60% of these deaths are from narcotic overdose. It is more likely that this coincides with middle school ages more so than late elementary school ages, but the point here is that it is never too early to talk to your children about drugs and their dangers. Narcotics are their own epidemic and outside the scope of this book, but adolescents are certainly facing this pressure significantly. There are many good books written on the subject of the narcotic epidemic, and it does impact children as well.

For reference, cancer deaths would be at number 3 on this list at 410 deaths.

Historical

For historical reference, *Our World in Data* reports that the mortality rate of children before age 15 was around 50% up until somewhere around 1900, when the global mortality rate dropped to 27% in 1950, and currently sits at around 4.3% globally.[7] Based on this, it was the rare exception rather than the norm that all of your children would make it to adulthood for the majority of human existence on this earth. Most deaths still occurred in children aged less than one, but deaths were higher in the older ages as well. Infectious disease ran rampant for much of human existence. Diseases such as smallpox, measles, diphtheria, cholera, pertussis (whooping cough), and scarlet fever were common and deadly. Some of the biggest advances in modern medicine include vaccines and antibiotics, which have drastically reduced the presence and mortality rates of these diseases. Other advances in medicine as well as better hygiene and nutrition in wealthier countries have aided in the improvement in childhood mortality.

Summary

Okay, so now we've gone over the data, and we've tried to focus it by age group. I've tried to point out what I think is significant. I hope this provides us a reasonable look at what we should fear and also reassures us how rare death in these age groups is. A lot of these should make sense to you, but some of them may surprise you. If it does surprise you, I hope it turns your attention to something that you may not have considered before.

The impetus for me writing this book is how anxious my wife is about harm to our children. She can get so wrapped up in small details sometimes that I think it can be overwhelming. Do you feel that way? Parenting certainly is overwhelming at times. But let's not let that get in our way of protecting our children from *serious* harm. Falls from the swing are certainly painful and can lead to costly trips to the ER if severe, but let's not get so wrapped up in preventing common childhood injuries that we fail to realize the true dangers to our children (Yes, I'm aware that falls from swings can kill children, but given the number of falls that happen every day, the likelihood is still exceedingly low). I have highlighted the common causes of death in children above, and the next chapters will be dedicated to helping you sort out how to take reasonable daily actions to prevent serious injury or death to hopefully reduce the stress of parenting. The truth is there are a few common ways your child could die, and there are many simple things you can do to reduce those chances.

* * *

References

1. Center for Disease Control and Prevention National Center for Injury Prevention and Control. Web-based Injury Statistics Query and Reporting System (WISQARS) [online]. Accessed August 6, 2024. https://wisqars.cdc.gov/lcd/?o=LCD&y1=2019&y2=2019&ct=10&cc=ALL&g=00&s=0&r=0&ry=2&e=0&ar=lcd1age&at=groups&ag=lcd2age&a1=0&a2=199

2. Korhonen V. Number of Children in the United States from 1950 to 2050. Statistica. Updated July 5, 2024. Accessed August 6,

2024, 2024. https://www.statista.com/statistics/457760/number-of-children-in-the-us/

3.The American Cancer Society medical and editorial content team. Key Statistics for Childhood Cancer. American Cancer Society. Updated May 28, 2024. Accessed August 6, 2024, 2024. https://www.cancer.org/cancer/types/cancer-in-children/key-statistics.html#:~:text=Childhood%20-cancer%20rates%20have%20been%20rising%20slightly%20-for,when%20the%205-year%20survival%20rate%20was%20about%2058%25.

4.Corwin M.D. M. Sudden infant death syndrome: Risk factors and risk reduction strategies. UpToDate. Updated March 13, 2024. Accessed August 13, 2024, 2024. https://www.uptodate.com/contents/sudden-infant-death-syndrome-risk-factors-and-risk-reduction-strategies

5.Choking Prevention for Babies & Children. HealthyChildren.org. Updated 8/23/2024. Accessed September 17, 2024. https://www.healthychildren.org/English/health-issues/injuries-emergencies/Pages/Choking-Prevention.aspx

6.Choking Hazards. Center for Disease Control. Updated February 25, 2022. Accessed August 14, 2024, 2024. https://www.cdc.gov/nutrition/InfantandToddlerNutrition/foods-and-drinks/choking-hazards.html

7.Roser M. Mortality in the past: every second child died. OurWorldInData.org. Accessed August 14, 2024, 2024. https://ourworldindata.org/child-mortality-in-the-past

Chapter 5

Automobiles

Thus far, we have explored how breakable the human body is, and I have introduced some of my own experiences as a foundation for explaining to you how the body is capable of healing from injury. This led us to the previous chapter, in which we discussed what is statistically most likely to actually *kill* your child in the modern world, focusing specifically on physical and bodily harm. In the following chapters, I will try to further clarify these causes of death and address appropriate measures to reduce the chances of death occurring to your child. This is the crux of this book. I hope the following chapters allow you to get the sense of how to focus on the things that matter most for preventing disaster for your child.

Recall chapter 3 when we discussed *Caveman Medicine*, or the events which the body of a child was developed to withstand in the natural world prior to modern technologies, like motorized vehicles for instance. Let's put that in perspective and take a bird's-eye view. Most of the things that are likely to kill your child in the modern world are not devices that would have been accessible to people 200 years ago. Certainly, riding on horseback as people have done for centuries has its dangers, but the most dangerous thing *any* of us do on a daily basis is get into a metal box with wheels on it and make those boxes go speeds that were unimaginable prior to the last 80 years. Motor vehicles and modern technologies have created entire fields of medicine and new research to treat the injuries associated with them. This includes ATVs, motorized boats (though non-motorized boats have been around for many millennia), golf carts, and other outdoor vehicles. Likewise, the safety prevention mechanisms have improved over time as well.

Of course, I must put this disclaimer here that children certainly can die from many things and that modern medicine has dramatically decreased the rates of death from infection sources. I am not brushing this off but rather looking more from the aspect of physical bodily harm.

No one is perfect, and if you've already been a parent for a while, you will understand how well parenting can draw attention to your flaws (so can marriage for that matter). Parenting is extremely tiring, and everyone has momentary lapses in judgment. The goal of the following chapters is to hit the highlights of three or so major rules for each "danger" that you really need to focus your efforts toward. If your child falls off the couch or if you cut a peanut butter and jelly sandwich into triangles when your son wanted rectangles, it does not matter in the long run. So, what are a few things we need to pay attention to and be on high alert? Parenting is ultimately a joy to be cherished, and parents of grown children love to comment on how fast it all goes by. So how can we put our energy into a few spots to allow ourselves time to enjoy (and often struggle through) the rest of it? Let's not miss the forest for the trees.

In surgery, the entire team in the operating room is required to stop what they are doing and perform what is called a surgical time-out. This includes reviewing a checklist on the most important parts of the surgery prior to starting. The aim is prevention of errors such as operating on the wrong person or the wrong limb. It occurs immediately prior to incision, and we make sure to identify the surgeon, the patient's name, date of birth, site and side of the surgical procedure, name of the surgical procedure, patient allergies, and the medications administered by the anesthesiologist. Some of the minor details may change from institution to institution, but the above are the essentials. It ensures that everyone is focused on what is actually about to happen and that we do not have any safety concerns before proceeding. In other words, it's the summary view of the surgery. I might not be focused on what anesthetic medications the anesthesiologist is administering just like he or she might not be focused on what size implant I intend to use during the patient's hip replacement. But there are a few things that *all* of us in the room need to be focused on and clarify. We hit on the essentials that matter for all of us to provide better safety for the patient. The airline industry uses a similar type of checklist prior to all flights. This has served to prevent many disasters. Why not try to take this type of behavior into the parenting world? What would be the focal points for child safety? We are going to try to point out the most important focal points for each possible danger. Here is the outline of the subsequent chapters:

- Chapter 5 - Automobiles
- Chapter 6 - Swimming Pools and Drowning
- Chapter 7 - Other Vehicles
- Chapter 8 - Falls
- Chapter 9 - Trampolines, Playgrounds, and Falls
- Chapter 10 - Choking/Suffocation
- Chapter 11 - Poison and Ingestion
- Chapter 12 - Firearms
- Chapter 13 - Fire Danger
- Chapter 14 - Homicide/Child Abuse
- Chapter 15 - Suicide
- Chapter 16 - Traumatic Brain Injury and Spinal Cord
- Chapter 17 - Lightning Strikes
- Chapter 18 - Animals and Allergies
- Chapter 19 - Deaths in the Developing World

Automobiles

One of the most common ways that any of us could die prior to age 45 is a motor vehicle crash. Traveling in cars is the most dangerous thing any of us do on a regular basis. It's even scarier to think of the age at which I will hand the keys over to my children and allow them to drive. Driving is so prevalent in our society that it has become second nature to many of us. There is no possible way to eliminate the risk of injury from driving completely, it just goes with the territory. I also do not think it is worth losing sleep over because the truth is most people do *not* suffer life threatening car wrecks despite millions of car travelers each day. Some things are just out of your control. Therefore, let's focus on what you *can* control with driving to reduce the risk of injury and death to your child as much as possible.

When my oldest son was four, we were on our way to the beach. About one mile into the trip, he called out to my wife and me and said, "hey I'm not buckled!" We had been so focused on packing the middle sections of the car and buckling our second son in at the time that we forgot to strap in our eldest. So maybe even I need to go back to step one, "start with buckling your child."

If I were to make a driving checklist, here's what I would include for every time you get into the car:

1. Make sure each child is secured *appropriately* (appropriate car seat/booster, buckled correctly, no bulky jackets/outer layers and check older children for seat belt buckling)
2. Ensure younger children do not have access to choking hazards
3. Do *not* start the car until you are either immediately leaving or intending to back the car out of the garage

Don't worry about what DVD you're going to put into the player, or if your child can reach their toy, or if your child has a snack, or if you need to get gas until you have done the things above. The rest you can worry about later or not at all. If your child cannot reach his pacifier, it may make for a noisy trip, but it won't kill him. Putting him in the wrong type of car seat might.

Why This Makes Me Nervous

Besides motor vehicle crashes being the overall largest source of harm for your child, I have seen the results of some potentially *preventable* deaths and disabilities in my personal medical experience. I have seen children with their spinal cords severed in half because they were improperly secured (and one of the parents was driving intoxicated in one of these incidents). This can happen if you buckle your undersized child without a booster in place or if you use the wrong sized car seat. I will admit that my view is skewed by seeing some of the worst of the worst, but if children come in with a severe injury after a car wreck, it is often related to improper restraint. I have seen patients come in where the parents had no physical injury and were discharged immediately whereas one of the children was left paralyzed from the neck down because of improper restraint. So, I emphasize this to you as I emphasize this to my wife and even myself: just take the time to make sure you do it right. No one wakes up thinking that they are going to intentionally wreck their car, but it happens. Children are remarkably resilient, and I have more commonly seen the opposite scenario from above, where parents are severely injured, but the children have little to no injury because of how well they are protected when properly fastened. Trust the car seat research when following instructions on how to install. It's a relatively simple thing to do.

To give you an idea why it is worth the time to review this chapter, an observational study in 2011 noted that 46% of car seats and booster seats are used incorrectly.[1,2] That number jumps to 59% when looking at car seats alone.[3] That means up to 59% of us are either installing the car seat incorrectly or buckling our children incorrectly! This includes loose installation, improper recline angle, and loose harness among others. Car seat use reportedly reduces risk for injury by up to 82% and booster seat use reduces risk for serious injury by 45% in children ages 4-8.[4] Also, 40% of children ages 8-12 killed in crashes were not buckled at all, and 31% of children less than age four killed in crashes were not buckled. Importantly, older children are more resistant to remaining in appropriate restraints throughout the trip.

Did I catch your attention yet? Car seat choice, booster seat choice, and maintenance of the seats are of critical value to your child's life in the event of a crash.

Choosing a Car Seat

All commercially available car seats in the United States are tested by the National Highway Traffic Safety Administration (NHTSA), and they must pass before they can be sold on the market. The NHTSA is a part of the U.S. Department of Transportation. For the latest recommendations on which car seat is appropriate for which child, you should visit their website at www.nhtsa.gov. There are four car seat restraint options: rear-facing only, forward-facing, booster seats, and seat belts. Some seats offer both rear-facing and forward-facing options in the same seat. The NHTSA has multiple tables that will direct you toward the appropriate type of car seat for your child depending on the age and weight.

Car seats are tested by the NHTSA with the Federal Motor Vehicle Safety Standard 213 (FMVSS) and the FVMSS 213a. The tests use anthropomorphic test devices (ATDs), i.e. crash test dummies, designed to mimic children at different ages. The standard 213 is for front impact and the 213a is for side impact.[5] The tests are standardized and the PDF file that outlines the exact process contains 153 pages as of August 2023, which I do not recommend reading unless you're extremely bored. The tests require video cameras that shoot at least 1000 frames per second for high-speed viewing as well as a slew of photographs that must be taken before and after testing. As you can imagine, there's a lot of physics involved as well. Frontal impact is tested as a deceleration (slowing down) of 30 mph as well as one at 20 mph. These decelerations take place in a period of less than 100 milliseconds. In layman's terms, they slam the car into a wall usually at 30 mph and watch in slow motion with test dummies. The side impact is tested at approximately 19.4 mph. All car seats sold in the US have passed the minimum requirements set forth by these tests.

Some major car seat review websites perform internal testing above and beyond the FMVSS standard. *Consumer Reports*, for example, has an internal crash protocol they perform at a lab. They test frontal impact at 35 mph and add some other nuances to better mimic real life situations. They state that their crash protection ratings are based on "(a) injury criteria measured on standardized child-sized dummies generally used in this type of simulated crash testing, (b) direct contact of the dummy's head with the simulated front seatback, and (c) a seat's ability to remain intact during the course of testing."[6] The most common cause of disabling injury or death in a child from a crash is a head injury, and the most common way for a head injury to occur is from the child's head striking the seat in front of it or the side of the vehicle. *Consumer Reports* reviews also review based on how well a car seat fits multiple vehicles and the ease of use of the seat, including installation. In their safety review, they claim to rate seats higher based on having a little extra "margin" in terms of going above and beyond the minimum qualifications for passing the NHTSA requirements. In other words, seats that perform better with less room for error get rated higher. There are other resources that rate car seats as well. If you are looking at purchasing a car seat, it's worth a look to find one in your price range, and I recommend reviewing the safety testing process that the reviewer is using.

It is important to point out that the price of the car seat does not make the car seat safer. Generally speaking, a higher car seat price may mean a nicer fabric or an easier way to secure the car seat to the car with more sophisticated buckle options. It may also mean a car seat can be easily transferred into a stroller or have cupholders. A higher price does *not* mean the car seat is safer. Laws regulate the sale of car seats, and they must meet safety criteria before they can be sold. As pointed out by the *Mom Loves Best* group, there are many affordable or free car seat options if you have limited financial resources.[7] Free car seats can be obtained through organizations including *Safe Kids Worldwide*, *Baby 2 Baby*, and *Everyday Miracles*. *Women, Infants, and Children* (WIC) and the *Department of Child Services* may also help. I recommend against purchasing used car seats. You do not know if the seat has been damaged or its condition, so you are taking a big risk. This is one childhood safety category you want to take very seriously. It only matters that you obtain a seat, not how expensive or "nice" it is.

Installing a Car Seat

Car seats are the bane of my existence, or at least they used to be prior to buying a minivan (yes, we are minivan people, and my wife looks sexy as hell in that thing). Many caretakers will agree with me. The easiest error to make in my personal experience is to not install the seat tightly enough. Often, I find that car seats slide over two inches from side to side while it should only move less than one inch from side to side or front to back when properly installed. This can be difficult to do the proper way.

When we were in residency, we purchased less expensive car seats. I'm a strong male, and I had difficulty installing car seat bases appropriately at times when I was by myself. It was often a two-person job, one to push the seat down hard and the other to pull the strap hard and tight. My wife can tell you that I cursed the most (sorry Mom and Dad) when installing car seats. It used to put me in a horrible mood, and I *absolutely loathed* switching them to another car. This is very much because I'm a perfectionist, and I like to go above and beyond when installing the car seat. Maybe this isn't the same for everyone, but it should probably wear you out when putting the car seat in appropriately. However, I will say some of the car seats we have purchased more recently for our older children are significantly easier to install, and we often chose budget friendly options when they were infants. More expensive car seats can be much easier to install.

Read the instructions carefully for each car seat you purchase, and I mean the whole booklet. I am liable to skip instructions for various objects that I purchase, but I don't play with my children's safety; I make sure I read the entire manual to understand exactly how all the parts work and what the manufacturer recommends. For newer parents (and ones that just need an occasional refresher), YouTube is the best place to look for education on how to properly install a car seat and how to appropriately buckle your child. If are installing a car seat by yourself and do not feel you are doing it well enough on your own, don't be afraid to recruit help. You can also do a web search for car seat classes or installations in your area. They are often available at health departments, fire departments, or hospitals.

To install a car seat correctly, follow the manufacturer's instructions. There are usually low anchor options and seat belt options. Check your vehicle owner's manual to ensure the car seat is compatible with options such as the Lower Anchors and Tethers for Children (LATCH) system before use. All commercial vehicles in the U.S. made after 2002 have LATCH available. In some vehicles, some car seats are more appropriate to use than others for car seat installation. The car seat should not move more than one inch from side-to-side or front-to-back.[8] To me, this step is critical and is one of the most overlooked when I am checking car seats before my children ride in them. Forward-facing seats have tether straps that can be anchored to the back of the seat, so use this option if it is compatible with your vehicle. Always install car seats on level ground and check the indicator on the car seat to make sure the car seat is installed at the correct angle. There may be a different appropriate angle on the car seat depending on if it's being installed for forward-facing or rear-facing or even booster mode versus harness mode.

Also, be sure to check the *other* car seats in which your child may ride. Your parents and other family members certainly care about your child immensely, but they are unlikely to put as much effort into researching safety as you will. Become an expert and make sure you assist with the installation of car seats in which your child will potentially ride. I always check the car seats that my parents or my in-laws install in their vehicles before letting my child go with them. They aren't going to put as much effort into it as I will. It's not because they don't care, it's because they haven't done the recent research like I've done to make it safe. Likewise, review appropriate harness techniques (chest clip height, how many fingers should you be able to fit, etc.) with your parents every so often. They may not have as much recent experience as you do with car seats, and car seats have changed since you were their young child.

Securing Your Child in the Car Seat

To appropriately secure your child[8]:

- Remove all bulky jackets and outer layers prior to placing your child in the seat
- Car seat straps should never be twisted
- Rear-facing seat straps should be at the slots that are either level with or just below your child's shoulders, while forward-facing harness straps should be level with or just above your child's shoulders.
- When placing your child in the seat, make sure the chest clip is level with the armpits.
- Make sure to appropriately tighten the straps. You should not be able to pinch any excess material of the strap at the shoulder.

My children often complain that they don't like me to buckle them because I make it tighter than Mom. This is one of the few things that I am *more* cautious than my wife about. What makes an orthopedic surgeon nervous? Car seats. I will never forget the first time I buckled a newborn into a car seat. I was so nervous because he looked so frail, and I made sure I studied up on how to adjust the car seat and watched multiple videos as if I were studying for a test.

Lastly, do not forget that heat strokes are a significant risk for children left in a car. Vehicles can heat very quickly in many weather conditions, and leaving windows cracked does not provide adequate ventilation. You should never leave your child unattended in a car, even for a short period of time.

Car Seat Maintenance

Car seats should be used according to the manufacturer's recommendations, which is why you should read the manual prior to the first time you install and use the car seat. Certain inserts cannot be removed. Strap covers and inserts should also not be added if specified in the manual. Also, the maximum lifespan of your car seat is usually printed on the car seat as an expiration date, and it will at least be specified in the manual. You can also find the answer on the manufacturer website. The typical maximum is 6 years. This ensures that the safety belts remain with appropriate friction and ensures new safety regulations and measures are updated with newer purchases. This usually becomes an issue when passing down a car seat from an older child to a younger child. Sometimes it's worth the new purchase. You should also register your car seat after purchase so that you will be contacted in the event of a safety recall or notice. I am guilty of not doing this for common appliances and purchases, but I always fill out the registration form when I purchase a car seat.

If you are ever in a crash, you may need to replace your car seat. The NHTSA recommends replacing car seats that have been involved in a "moderate to severe crash."[9] Car seats may still be used if involved in a minor crash, which is defined by the NHTSA as having to include all five of the following:

- The vehicle was able to be driven away from the crash site
- The vehicle door nearest the car seat was not damaged
- None of the passengers in the vehicle sustained any injuries in the crash
- If the vehicle has airbags, the airbags did not deploy during the crash
- There is no visible damage to the car seat.

If any of those five definitions are not met, the car seat should be replaced.

Likewise, when you are disposing of a car seat because of age or damage, manufacturers recommend cutting the straps, slicing the seat, and/or writing on the seat with a permanent marker.[10] This protects someone else from obtaining your expired seat. Some retailers may offer car seat recycling programs from time to time, so I recommend doing an internet search before you take it to the landfill. Donation companies such as Goodwill do not accept car seats or baby walkers for these reasons.

Rear-Facing vs. Forward-Facing

As for when to switch from rear-facing to forward-facing, some of this is dictated by state law, so check your state's laws prior to making the decision to switch. Typically, the decision is made based on age, weight, and height of the child. Likewise, make sure that your child's height and weight are appropriate for your car seat per the manufacturer. Our children were *miserable* car riders before age 2. We batted zero out of four for peaceful car riders. Some of our friends would tell us how their children just fell asleep and didn't make a peep during six-hour car trips. Our children would nap for thirty minutes maximum and then throw massive fits the rest of the way. We turned our car seats around at age two because they had met the appropriate height and weight requirements for our car seat, and they all seemed to be better entertained when forward facing. Also, in my old Jeep, our children became cramped when they reached a certain height because of the mismatch of the car seat relative to the adult seat. They ended up sitting in a frog leg position because the Jeep seats just were not made for car seats the same way that our van's seats are. Though we switched at two years of age based on the weight and height recommendations of our seats, the American Academy of Pediatrics (AAP) recommends staying rear-facing as long as possible. If your children are able to sit comfortably in a rear-facing seat, keep them rear-facing until they cannot.[11] The AAP makes many policy statements about various childhood safety and health topics and periodically updates them with new evidence over time. They also make a fantastic guide for car seats located at www.healthychildren.org/carseatguide. I recommend a visit.

Rear-facing car seats are more protective of younger children, supported by recently published data.[12] Biomechanical data supports this as well. The advantages of rear-facing car seats have to do with the head, rib cage, and pelvis of younger children, particularly less than age four.[13] Infants' and younger children's heads are relatively larger than their necks compared with adults. Combined with the relatively weaker spinal muscles, the head and neck flex more forward and downward compared to adults if the child is forward-facing. Likewise, the rib cage and pelvis are softer at younger ages because of their cartilage-heavy structure. They do not have the same strength of fully developed bony structures in older children and adults. Therefore, a shoulder belt and lap belt will not provide the same restraint in younger children and infants and will allow more dangerous forces on these structures as well as the neck. Rear-facing seats protect the pelvis and rib cage better by transferring energy to the pelvis by the seat back rather than the seat belt.

Booster Seat Rules

Always check your state laws prior to switching, but in general you should switch from a car seat to a booster when your child outgrows the limit for height or weight on your car seat.

Your child may transition to using a regular seat belt when they are big enough, typically recommended at 4 feet and 9 inches in height and between ages 8-12. According to the NHTSA, for a seat belt to work properly, it must fit correctly. The lap belt should lie snugly across the upper thighs and not the stomach. The shoulder belt should fit snugly across the chest and shoulder and not the face or neck. Back seats are also safer than front seats for children.[14] I have personally witnessed severe injuries in children who were not seated in booster seats when they should have been. You don't want this to happen to your child.

Backless vs. Highbacked Booster Seats

One of the biggest battles we have with our eldest is his desire to sit in a backless booster seat. We purchased a car seat that serves as both a five-point harness and a high-back booster, and when it was time, we started allowing him to use the regular seatbelt. We did extensive research on this prior to this decision. High-backed booster seats are safer, and it was that simple. They provide extra protection for side impact because they provide head and neck support that backless boosters do not.[13,15] In our minds, more safety is better, despite it being more of a hassle for him to buckle compared with a backless booster. This being said, I used keep a backless booster in the trunk of my sedan (prior to purchasing a larger vehicle) because it was small and easy to keep in the car if I needed to pick our son up from school. Backless boosters are also significantly cheaper. Based on the available research, children should ride in a high back booster until they outgrow it.[15-17]

As far as a 5-point harness versus a seatbelt in a high-back booster, there are no studies that I could find that actually compare the two. You at least want your child to be able to secure the seatbelt and wear it appropriately, especially if they fall asleep during the drive. As long as they can be appropriately secured, both the 5-point harness and shoulder and lap belt are equally safe options. Likewise, check that your child has buckled before leaving your driveway (Checklist step one!). Do not be like me the time I made sure to pack the car for a vacation but forgot to secure my eldest, or else it doesn't matter.

Vehicle Maintenance

I gave you a checklist for each individual trip, but what about the long haul? It is equally important to consider the condition of your vehicle. Car maintenance can be expensive, but it is well worth it for safety purposes. Your best bet is to set reminders every 3, 6, and 12 months for normal car maintenance, including oil changes, tire rotation, tire replacement (tire blowouts are dangerous), and brakes. These are easy things you can do to reduce your stress about car wrecks.

It is also worth discussing the age of your vehicle. New vehicles have gotten increasingly expensive, but you might want to consider an upgrade if you have an older vehicle and can afford a newer one. Think of it as the price of safety for your child. Another website that tracks data is *Our World in Data*.[18] This website pulls data from the *Institute for Health Metrics and Evaluation* (IMHE), among others. This is a global health statistic tracking institute at the University of Washington in Seattle. This website has graph data that you can parse out by country or by the globe. In children ages 5 to 14 in the year 2019, they list 935 deaths by road accident, which is less than cancer overall at 1,121. If you travel back to 1990, there were 2,296 deaths by road accident and 1,420 deaths by cancers. That is a drop of more than 50% in road accident deaths in a 29-year period! If you scroll through, you can see road accidents drop in number almost yearly from 1990 to 2010 before it stabilizes at the number less than 50%. So, what happened in that 20-year period? Did fewer people drive? No, the population has only increased. The major advances are airbag safety, car seat safety, car safety, and probably awareness as well. Maybe the advances in safety are worth the trade in for your 15-year-old vehicle for a newer one. By the way, driving drowsy can make you more likely to crash, so vehicles with lane assist and collision avoidance can only help if you get drowsy at the wheel.

    I will go out of my way here to make an unnecessary plug for minivans because I mentioned that we have one earlier. I have had discussions over the years with many people who refuse to even test drive minivans because they don't want to be tempted. They are the greatest cars for toting children. If only there were a car literally made to shuttle kids! If only there were a car made to allow getting children in and out of a car more easily or to install car seats more easily! If only there were a car designed with child safety in mind as well as the ability to have three rows at a reasonably affordable price! Oh wait, they make those; they're called minivans. Minivans are much cheaper than some other three row competitors, especially SUVs. Our Honda Odyssey has lane assist among other driving assist features, has a built-in screen, has seats that are completely removable or foldable to make more room, and has sliding middle row seats (the best feature in my opinion). I can even open the car doors at the school pick-up line with a button from my driver seat, and it will not allow the car door to shut on a child's limb. Sliding doors also make it less likely for your child to swing the door out in a parking lot and ding a neighboring car. No, they are not made to be sexy, but they are literally *made* with children in mind. Remember how minivans worked when we were children in the 80s and 90s? Well, they took those concepts and made it even better and more specialized. The minivan makers know their game is not to make the car look especially flashy but to have the most ridiculously awesome features to make it easier to drive kids around, and they do it way better than they did 20 years ago. I seriously recommend (no medical advice to this one) checking one out if you have multiple children. The features are unmatched by any other type of vehicle, and it drives very well to boot.

Impaired or Distracted Driving

You would think this paragraph goes without saying, but safe driving is extremely important, and I know I am guilty of not driving my best when the children are in the car at times. Though speeding can be dangerous, *defensive* driving is a more important focus for safety. If you pretend that the other drivers on the road don't know what they're doing, I think you're less likely to have an accident. In other words, always check twice before turning right on red, be cautious about going through yellow lights or accelerating immediately after the light turns green, etc. I believe other drivers are more likely to hurt you than you are to hurt yourself, so just be cautious. Do *not* use a cell phone to text while driving. With modern car features and phone features, voice texting is easy and it's not worth the risk to you or your child. Do not let yourself be distracted by things other than phones either. This includes trying to eat while driving, putting on makeup, reaching back toward your children, and other distracting tasks.

Do not drive while intoxicated. To reinforce this concept, I will refer to the safety resource on the CDC website. I'm going to quote their statistics here. The following facts are adopted from this page.[19] In 2020, alcohol impaired driving, either the driver of the same car or the opposing car, was involved in 24% of deaths in children ages 14 and younger. In that same age group, when there was a child fatality in car crash, alcohol impaired drivers were less likely to restrain their children at 56% of the fatalities versus 38% of non-alcohol related fatalities. So not only are you more likely to crash if you drive impaired, but you are also simultaneously less likely to restrain your child appropriately (although this may just go with the combination of a parent being of poor judgment if they are going to drive drunk anyway). Even one drink could impair you enough to make a mistake, and it's better to take turns with your spouse on who gets a margarita that night at the Mexican restaurant than take a risk. Driving under the limit for your state might be legal, but it does not mean that it is maximally safe.

Drowsy Driving

This one is probably more common for some parents than others, but driving while drowsy is also very dangerous. In some cases, it is as dangerous or more dangerous than driving while intoxicated to the legal limit. Yes, you read that correctly. If you have a few drinks and drive past the legal limit, you will be arrested. If you drive on four hours of sleep, despite being just as physically impaired as an intoxicated driver, there is no law for this. I will thank Matthew Walker, PhD, for this segment. I recently read his book *Why We Sleep*, and it was certainly eye opening. I heartily recommend this book for your general health. Regardless, one of his most powerful segments in the book highlights a lot of the data with sleep deprived driving. One of his references is a study by AAA[20], which shows that over a 24-hour period, if you sleep 6-7 hours, you have 1.3 times the crash rate than someone who sleeps more than 7 hours. It goes to 1.9 (almost double!) the crash rate with 5-6 hours of sleep and 4.3 times the crash rate at 4-5 hours of sleep. That's with a one-night trend, let alone stacking multiple nights of poor sleep in a row. If you *usually sleep* for 4-5 hours per day, your rate may be 5.4 times higher. And we all know how easy it is to get sleep when you have a newborn.

The scariest comparison to me is with alcohol intoxication. I think everyone would agree that driving at or above the legal limit is an incredibly risky (and stupid) thing to do for many reasons. You would never drive drunk (or at least you would think that you wouldn't, but I've seen unfortunate victims of this) with children in your car, and hopefully never by yourself either. I recommend avoiding even one drink if you are planning to drive with your children in the car. But I'm sure very few of us recognize that driving on sleep deprivation could potentially be *just as dangerous* as driving while intoxicated. If that doesn't catch your attention, then I don't know what will. If you notice that you are getting sleepy while driving, say long distance for example, then it's best to quickly find a hotel or take turns with a licensed passenger in the car. This poses a serious health risk to you and your children, so take it seriously. Sleep matters and is an incredibly important part of our health, so don't neglect it, especially at the potential cost of your children.[21]

Backing the Car Out

Carbon monoxide poisoning is a potential risk for your child with vehicles if you're not paying attention. *Never* leave a vehicle running in a garage. Period. This includes if the garage door is open. If you want to load your children into the car first so that you can take a few minutes to finish getting yourself ready without having to worry about them killing one another, that's perfectly fine. We do it all the time. But if you need to do this, back the car out of the garage if you're going to start the ignition. It's a simple safety rule that works.

Carbon monoxide is an odorless gas that is released by combustion engines. If left in a confined space, like the garage, the gas can become trapped and get into the lungs. Carbon monoxide competes for oxygen binding sites in the blood stream, so it inhibits the ability of your lungs to exchange and deliver oxygen to the body. This can lead to death in some circumstances.

On cool days while the van is parked in the garage, we will leave our doors open, and we never leave the children unattended for more than a few minutes after securing them. Do NOT leave your children in a hot car unattended. Infants especially are at risk for heat injury. Be sure to count your children in the car to make sure you have all of them before leaving and use your backup camera if you have one.

Summary

If you're paying attention to what I'm saying here, why would you *not* take this seriously? Just make the checklist a part of your routine. Make sure you know how to properly install a car seat and check it every few months to make sure it's not loose. Make sure you are putting the child in correctly because according to the above statistics, you more than likely are not. It's simple. Refer to a good video from an instructor and/or a website with good information, such as the NHTSA or healthychildren.org. Make sure your parents and the other caretakers for your children are doing the same. If you do this, you don't have to stress about it. You've done what you can to control what you can control. I've seen firsthand the results of improper restraint. Don't let yourself become this statistic. I don't worry as much about my children falling from monkey bars. I do worry about making sure the car seat straps are tight and appropriately positioned in the car every time.

* * *

References

1. Greenwall NK. National Child Restraint Use Special Study (Traffic Safety Facts Research Note. Report No. DOT HS 812 157). *National Highway Traffic Safety Administration.* June 2015 (August 14, 2024)

2. Greenwall NK. Results of the national child restraint use special study. (Report No. DOT HS 812 142). *National Highway Traffic Safety Administration.* May 2015

3. Raymond P, Searcy S, Findley D. Additional analysis of National Child Restraint Use Special Study: Child restraint misuse (Traffic Safety Facts Research Note. Report No. DOT HS 812 527. *National Highway Traffic Safety Administration.* July 2018

4. Preventing Child Passenger Injury. Center for Disease

Control: Child Passenger Safety. Updated May 16, 2024. Accessed August 14, 2024, https://www.cdc.gov/child-passenger-safety/prevention/?CDC_AAref_Val=https://www.cdc.gov/transportationsafety/child_passenger_safety/cps-factsheet.html

5.Laboratory Test Procedure for FMVSS No. 213 Child Restraint Systems & FMVSS No. 213a Child Restraint Systems - Side Impact Protection. *US Department of Transportation National Highway Traffic Safety Administration.* August 23, 2023. https://www.nhtsa.gov/sites/nhtsa/files/2023-10/TP-213-11-10272023.pdf

6.How Consumer Reports Tests Child Car Seats. Consumer Reports. Updated March 12, 2020. Accessed August 25, 2024. https://www.consumerreports.org/car-seats/how-consumer-reports-tests-child-car-seats/

7.Gardiner K. How to Get a Free Baby Car Seat: 9 Clever Options. Mom Loves Best. Updated February 10, 2024. Accessed August 25, 2024. https://momlovesbest.com/how-to-get-free-car-seats#:~:text=1%20Free%20car%20seats%20can%20be%20obtained%20through,find%20free%20or%20affordable%20car%20seats.%20More%20items

8.Keeping Kids Safe: A Parent's Guide to Protecting Children In and Around Cars. U.S. Department of Transportation National Highway Traffic Safety Administration; 2017. https://www.nhtsa.gov/sites/nhtsa/files/documents/13237-parents_guide_playing_it_safe_tagged_0.pdf

9.Car Seat Use After a Crash. U.S. Department of Transportation National Highway Traffic Safety Administration. Accessed August 25, 2024. https://www.nhtsa.gov/car-seats-and-booster-seats/car-seat-use-after-crash

10.Jondle J. Do You Have an Expired Car Seat? Here's Why It Matters. Healthline. Updated September 17, 2019. Accessed August 25, 2024. https://www.healthline.com/health/baby/car-seat-expiration

11.Durbin DR, Hoffman BD, Council On Injury V, Poison P.

Child Passenger Safety. *Pediatrics.* Nov 2018;142(5)doi:10.1542/peds.2018-2460

12. Anderson DM, Peterson RW. Rear-facing child safety seat effectiveness: evidence from motor vehicle crash data. *Inj Prev.* Aug 2023;29(4):320-326. doi:10.1136/ip-2022-044815

13. Brolin K, Stockman I, Andersson M, Bohman K, Gras L-L, Jakobsson L. Safety of Children in cars: A review of biomechanical aspects and human body models. *International Association of Traffic and Safety Sciences.* 2015;(38):92-102.

14. Car Seat Recommendations for Children. U.S. Department of Transportation National Higway Traffic Safety Administration; 2019. https://www.nhtsa.gov/sites/nhtsa.gov/files/documents/carseat-recommendations-for-children-by-age-size.pdf

15. Car Seats and Booster Seats. U.S. Department of Transportation National Highway Traffic Safety Administration. Accessed August 27, 2024. https://www.nhtsa.gov/vehicle-safety/car-seats-and-booster-seats

16. Fox H. High back booster seats: why our tough crash tests matter. Which? Expert testing, reviews and advice. Updated June 21, 2020. Accessed August 27, 2024. https://www.which.co.uk/news/article/high-back-booster-seats-why-our-crash-tests-matter-a9E875u4e7Pp#:

~:text=For%20older%20children%2C%20the%20best%20type%20of%20seat,padded%20wings%20provide%20protection%20during%20a%20side-on%20collision.

17. Thomas E. The Benefits of Keeping the Back on Your Booster Seat. Consumer Reports. Updated October 7, 2021. Accessed August 27, 2024. https://www.consumerreports.org/babies-kids/car-seats/keep-the-back-on-your-booster-seat-a4806370987/

18. Causes of death in children aged 5 to 14, United States, 2021. Our World in Data. Accessed August 27, 2024. https://ourworldindata.org/grapher/causes-of-death-in-5-14-year-olds?time=latest&country=~USA

19. Child Passenger Safety: Risk Factors for Child Passengers.

Center for Disease Control. Updated May 16, 2024. Accessed August 27, 2024. https://www.cdc.gov/child-passenger-safety/risk-factors/?CDC_AAref_Val=https://www.cdc.gov/transportationsafety/child_passenger_safety/cps-factsheet.html

20. Tefft BC. Acute Sleep Deprivation and Risk of Motor Vehicle Crash Involvement (Technical Report). AAA Foundation for Traffic Safety. Accessed September 17, 2024. https://aaafoundation.org/acute-sleep-deprivation-risk-motor-vehicle-crash-involvement/

21. Tefft B. Acute Sleep Deprivation and Risk of Motor Vehicle Crash Involvement. AAA Foundation. Updated December 2016. Accessed August 27, 2024. https://aaafoundation.org/acute-sleep-deprivation-risk-motor-vehicle-crash-involvement/

Chapter 6

Swimming Pools and Drowning

This is the one that gives me the most anxiety as a parent and as a physician. I can mend broken bones, even bad ones, but I cannot fix a drowned child. The truth is the only way to avoid drowning is appropriate awareness when you are near a potential danger. When we are near a swimming pool, especially when staying on the property of a family member with one in the back yard, I do not rest easy.

Drowning is the number one cause of death in children ages 1-4. Think about that for a minute. Water is the biggest danger to your child in this age group, not trampolines or playgrounds. It is the second leading cause of unintentional death in children ages 5-14. The CDC webpage on drowning also states that for every fatal drowning for children under the age of 18, another 7 receive ER care for nonfatal drowning.[1] That should scare you as well. Nonfatal car wrecks sometimes cause permanent disability for a child, but usually not. Nonfatal drowning can *severely* affect your child's brain. Over 65% of drownings happen in bathtubs in infants under the age of one. The most common location for drowning for children ages 1-4 is a swimming pool. In ages 5-14, 30% of drownings happen in swimming pools and 40% occur in natural bodies of water according to the CDC.

My in-laws had a pool at their old house. Although it was located in their backyard through two sets of locked doors and a stairwell leading down to a patio, it still made me nervous. We visit my wife's grandparents a lot as well. They have a pool, and our boys frequently roam on their property. Let me tell you, I watch the pool like a hawk. Despite this, I have a very vivid memory of the time my second son got into a pool without his "floaties" on. We were living at a rental house for a year, and the neighborhood pool opened for the summer. It had been at least 8 months since my son had been in a pool, so he forgot that he needed to have floaties on prior to entering the pool. I walked in with my oldest two children and a bag. While I was setting the bag down to get his floaties and sunscreen, my eldest grabbed me and told me that my second son was drowning. I turned around and, sure enough, he had gone down the steps into the pool and was underwater. Luckily, he was only under for a few seconds, but that's all it takes if you have a lapse in attention.

The biggest safety tips I can give you:

- Teach your child how to swim when old enough
- Teach your child how to call for help and how dangerous pools are
- Use floatation devices when appropriate
- Be extra vigilant
- Set up pool safeguards (if it's your pool)
- Learn CPR (just in case)

The reality of drowning is that it can happen *quickly*. I want you to hold your breath for as long as you can. Now remember that a child's lungs are significantly smaller than yours, and a child cannot hold their breath probably more than 15 to 30 seconds at best. That would be when they are *trying* to hold their breath. When they get under the water, they may panic and start inhaling water immediately. The truth is that you often have a few minutes to get them out of the water and have a chance at revival, but even a few minutes of lack of oxygen to the brain can impair the brain for life. This is the part where you just plain have to pay attention. The most vulnerable children are those at ages who are learning to swim but not great swimmers, but all are potentially at risk. They are dangerous enough to think they can swim better than they actually can. You must also keep direct vision on children at all times. Drowning can be a silent event because the child gets under the water and can never get their mouth back up to call for help.

For children who cannot swim, or if swimming in the ocean or other natural body of water, I recommend you pick a floatation device that is U.S. Coast Guard (USCG) approved. The USCG ensures that personal flotation devices (PFDs) are put through recognized laboratory testing, and you can trust that it has been put through its paces. We have a rule for our non-swimmers that the floaties have to be on *and* a grownup has to be in the pool with them prior to entering. For our second son who is learning to swim, an adult must be in the pool for him to jump in, and we punish this very harshly because of how serious it is to us. Floatation devices are not foolproof, however, and they still require supervision. It's best to be at arm's length for younger children and to always have a direct visual on a child.

Swimming Pools

Pools can be a great source of fun for children, but they can also be a source of great danger. There are two distinct scenarios to be aware of drowning potential: a child wandering into a pool unseen, and a child drowning in a pool during a swimming episode. Given the difference, some of the following will be more relevant to keeping your child out of a nearby pool by setting up safeguards while other tips will be more relevant to monitoring for drowning and prevention during pool play time.

There's not a lot of data on the exact circumstances in which children drown in pools, but I can speak on this anecdotally and inferentially. One possibility is a child escaping unseen and ending up in the pool. It may be that the child either slips in because they get too close or that they forget they cannot swim. It may be that the child thinks of the pool as a fun place to be without knowledge of danger because they've never had a safety issue when you are with them in the pool. They might also see a toy in the pool they want. You might be in another part of the yard, or you may not have realized the child has left the house, and all it takes is a few minutes.

I think another common scenario occurs when there are multiple adults socializing in an area. This is particularly dangerous because everyone assumes that someone else is watching the children. Socializing around the pool is a distraction, so keep your focus on your child. Clarify with the adults who is going to be watching each child. Don't assume someone else, even your spouse, is watching your child automatically. If you need to get up for a quick break, clarify with verbal acknowledgement and eye contact from another responsible adult prior to leaving. Be careful about drinking alcohol when monitoring your child; know your limits. Also, just because a lifeguard is present doesn't mean they are flawless at catching every child the moment they start drowning. No one watches your own child like you do.

Bathtubs

Let us not forget bathtubs as a source of drowning. One AAP source states that bathtubs are responsible for 62-71% of infant drownings and buckets are responsible for 16%.[2] The best option is prevention, and the best prevention is to remain beside the bathtub at *all* times. Drowning can happen even while you walk down the hall to get a towel. If you need to do a quick chore, get your child out of the tub and take them with you after you've finished bathing them. Yes, young children love playing in the bath, but if you don't have the time to sit with them to watch, get them out. Do not leave them unattended. Reportedly children can drown in as little as one inch of water, which includes splash pads, puddles, and toilets.[3]

Natural Bodies of Water

Natural bodies of water become more dangerous to children as they get older. This is due partly to more exposure with age, but also due to overconfidence in their ability to swim. Children, and even adults for that matter, do not recognize how different swimming in a pool is from swimming in a current. I've witnessed an adult panic and almost drown in a river current before, and it was terrifying. Many adults die each year in rip currents in the ocean. Children are even weaker swimmers. As for children, the three best things you can do are to: educate your child about the dangers and reiterate them every time you get into a natural body of water, consider making them get in with a flotation device as a precaution, and keep your eye on them. If you are at a beach with warning flags about currents, do not ignore them. Check danger levels for swimming each day you are going to swim in an ocean. Many beaches have a flag system with different colors signaling different warnings about the current and conditions. Education and surveillance are the keys here.

Adult Supervision

The AAP technical report on the *Prevention of Drowning* from 2021 suggests that it is difficult to define "adequate supervision" from adults[4] though it is often cited as a contributing factor to childhood drowning events. They cite a description of supervision being composed of 3 components: proximity, attention, and continuity. Proximity means how close you are to the child, but there are variable levels of proximity. For instance, being close enough to touch your child at arm's reach at all times in the pool is different than being outside the pool with a line of sight. Attention and continuity are all about awareness of the situation, and that's what's hard to address. You must be aware and make decisions that will lower the likelihood of you missing a drowning episode. For example, if you are supposed to be monitoring your child in the pool, maybe it is best to never touch your cell phone, even if it's to make a phone call. You may think you can provide adequate attention while talking on the phone, but that is not always the case. Even the best of us makes mistakes and have lapses in attention. Likewise, self-reported caregiver alcohol use has been shown to predict higher likelihood of injury occurrence and higher injury severity, with increasing chances with the number of beverages consumed.[5] This is true for all sources of nonintentional injury in children, not just swimming. It's best not to drink alcohol when swimming with children in the pool.

The Silence of Drowning

As stated earlier, drowning is often a quiet event. If a child is able to yell for help, they are more likely to be noticed and get the assistance they need. However, most children are not able to do this because their mouth gets underwater, and they cannot come up to speak. They usually cannot splash either by the time they realize they need help. One of the most haunting pictures I have in my head is of my second son being submerged underneath the water with his eyes looking at me, trying to get his mouth above water. Though it was only a few seconds, and he did not have any medical consequences, that mental picture sticks with me and terrifies me, and it happened while I was putting my bag down and getting a bottle of sunscreen out. My eldest was the one who saw it, and I am glad he was there. If you are within arm's reach of your child at all times in a body of water with a direct visualization, you will be able to recognize drowning situations more reliably and quickly.

Swim Lessons

Teaching your child to swim is, perhaps, the best way to prevent drowning. Infants are not able to swim, but there is a group called Infant Swimming Resource (ISR) who will provide lessons for infants and young children. The lessons mostly focus on teaching infants to roll onto their backs to float until help can reach them. As far as I could find, there is no evidence that lessons at this young of an age make a difference in drowning potential for infants and toddlers, so I cannot recommend specifically for or against these types of lessons. We did not use ISR for our children. In fact, research is mixed on exposures to chlorination products in pools at younger ages, with some suggestion that it may predispose a child to asthma and/or bronchitis and other allergic conditions.[6,7] However, a study from 2011 showed the opposite, that asthma risk may be lower and lung function may be improved from early exposure.[8] Therefore, the evidence is mixed on infant exposure to pool chemicals for long term consequences. Regardless, swimming lessons at any age are not an absolute protection against drowning, and they are certainly not a substitute for adult supervision.

One study reports that the average age for a child to be developmentally ready to swim and to develop the appropriate motor skills is 4.5 years.[9] Children as young as three might benefit from swim lessons, but four appears to be the best age to start.[10] Swim lessons have been shown to reduce the risk of fatal drowning.[4] The AAP supports swim lessons for children older than age one. I highly recommend swim lessons, at least by age 5. Get them in the pool and get them practicing as much as possible with supervision. The more they practice, the better they will do. Get them comfortable with the pool, but also get them comfortable with the *rules*. Make sure they know how to call for help or swim to the side of the pool. Make sure your children know not to wrestle in the pool or climb on each other. Also, teach them to watch out for each other and to never swim alone. Seizure disorder can also severely increase the risk of your child drowning, estimated up to 20 fold higher risk, so be aware of this special circumstance.[11]

If you are going to enroll your child in swim lessons under the age of three, the AAP recommends the guidelines proposed by the World Aquatic Babies and Children Network[4]:

1. Required parental involvement
2. Fun atmosphere with one-one-one teaching
3. Qualified teachers
4. Warm water to prevent hypothermia (child's body temperature becoming too low),
5. Maintenance of water purity
6. A limited number of submersions to prevent water ingestion and hyponatremia (a severe electrolyte/hydration problem).

It must be stated again, swim lessons are not a substitute for adult supervision. Though they certainly help with prevention, they are not at all foolproof. It's also worth mentioning that you might do well to go to a class on rescuing a drowning child. There are many cases in which a relative has entered a natural body of water, such as a lake or ocean, and the relative dies in the process of saving the child, or both die.[12] At the very minimum, you should burn it into your mind that you should always call for help before entering the water to rescue someone, and you should have a flotation device if entering and open body of water. Swimming in an open body of water is highly dangerous by itself, but it is monumentally more difficult when trying to rescue someone. I've witnessed a near-drowning event of an adult in a river, and the only thing that saved the day was some children with some floatation devices that were on the shoreline. It doesn't matter how strong you think you are or how good of a swimmer you might be. I personally have not taken such a class, like a lifeguard class, but I know to grab a flotation device before entering an open body of water.

Secondary or Dry Drowning

What about "secondary drowning" or "dry drowning"? These are not really medical terms, but the idea behind the terms is a child develops delayed respiratory or breathing symptoms, even though they are no longer in the water. This would be a presentation after inhaling a lot of water in a near drowning event. In reality, *dry* or *secondary drowning* is a delayed presentation of lung complications. Essentially, it happens as a near drowning event in which the child clears their lungs eventually, but the lungs swell over time from the trauma and irritation from water in their lungs. A review of 75 pediatric patients admitted to a hospital for secondary drowning showed that all pulmonary (lung) symptoms developed within 8 hours of the near drowning event.[13] I've heard some people mention 24 hours when discussing secondary drowning, but research supports that you would know within 8 hours by a severe cough, wheezing, or other difficulties with breathing. This may be accompanied by a fast breathing rate, vomiting, or a change in mental status.[14] These symptoms will at least *start* within 8 hours, but they may worsen over 24 hours. There have been some social media and news induced fears about *dry drowning* occurring days after an insult, but this is a medical myth. Regardless, the main point is that you should *always* have your child evaluated emergently by a medical professional in a near drowning event.

CPR

Cardiopulmonary Resuscitation (CPR) is a vital tool for survival if a drowning event has occurred. I highly recommend every parent or caregiver attend a CPR class and review the protocols from time to time to stay up to date. According to references cited by the AAP technical report, early bystander CPR has the greatest effect on survival and preservation of brain function after a drown victim is pulled from the water.[4] The main function of the lungs is to exchange oxygen into the blood stream, and the main function of the heart is to pump that oxygen into the various organs and limbs of our bodies. If either of these processes stop, the brain will start to die. If a drowning victim still has a pulse, then respiratory support alone is required, meaning rescue breaths or "mouth-to-mouth" to allow oxygen exchange. If a pulse is not present, then chest compressions must be added to circulate blood because the heart is no longer doing its job effectively. Chest compressions without rescue breaths are not enough. If you do happen to witness an event, the child must be evaluated at an Emergency Department (ED) emergently, even if the child resumes breathing and spontaneously regains consciousness. One study from 2020 showed that survival with better neurologic (brain) function was associated with bystander compressions and ventilations as a part of CPR in children ages 5-15 compared with compression-only CPR[15]

The American Heart Association (AHA) provides CPR classes in many locations throughout the U.S. Access their CPR webpage at: cpr.heart.org. They have links to find CPR classes as well as downloadable charts for reference. There are multiple CPR instructional videos on YouTube as well, although a formal class is best.

Pool Safeguards for Owners

Lastly, if you or your family member own a pool, make sure appropriate safeguards are in place. One study shows four-sided isolation fences reduce a child's risk of drowning by 83% compared to a three-sided fence (i.e. does not separate the house from the pool).[16] Make sure gates and doors are closed and locked so your child cannot sneak out of the house (probably a great idea even if you *don't* own a pool). Fence gates should be self-closing and self-latching. Pool alarms that will sound if something falls into the water can be purchased as well. Take these precautions seriously. All it takes is one small lapse in judgment or caution and a small amount of time. Lock any gates surrounding your pool so other children cannot get into your yard. Though pool covers are good in theory, they lack the same supporting evidence as fencing and have not been shown to prevent drowning.[4] In addition to the mental burden you would have to live with for the rest of your life if someone else's child drowned in your pool, you can also potentially be held criminally or civilly liable.

The U.S. Consumer Product Safety Commission (CPSC) publishes multiple safety resources for families and homeowners. They have one specifically entitled *Safety Barrier Guidelines for Residential Pools, Preventing Child Drownings.*[17] This includes recommendations for fence height, door alarms, pool covers, and others. I highly recommend reviewing this if you or a close family member owns a pool. You might even find helpful tips, such as fences with vertical bars being superior to chain link because of children being able to more easily climb chain link fences.

Summary

The summary for this section is that you need to always keep an eye on your children near bodies of water. Drowning happens quickly, and close observation is the best prevention. If you own a pool, make sure it is appropriately surrounded by a fence, ideally with four sides, and has a pool alarm. Cover it when not in use if possible. If you have young children and are purchasing a new house or moving to a new rental, it is probably best to avoid a house with a pool if possible. It's better to know a good friend with a pool or go to a community pool. Pools make me more nervous than anything else I'll mention in this book with respect to my own children at their current ages.

* * *

References

1. Drowning Prevention: Summer Swim Safety. Center for Disease Control Drowning Prevention. Updated May 9, 2024. Accessed

August 27, 2024. https://www.cdc.gov/drowning/prevention/summer-swim-safety.html

2. Denny SA, Quan L, Gilchrist J, et al. Prevention of Drowning. *Pediatrics*. May 2019;143(5)doi:10.1542/peds.2019-0850

3. Drowning Prevention for Curious Toddlers: What Parents Need to Know. HealthyChildren.org. Updated 6/29/2023. Accessed September 18, 2024. https://www.healthychildren.org/English/safety-prevention/at-play/Pages/Water-Safety-And-Young-Children.aspx

4. Denny SA, Quan L, Gilchrist J, et al. Prevention of Drowning. *Pediatrics*. Aug 2021;148(2)doi:10.1542/peds.2021-052227

5. Damashek A, Williams NA, Sher K, Peterson L. Relation of caregiver alcohol use to unintentional childhood injury. *J Pediatr Psychol*. May 2009;34(4):344-53. doi:10.1093/jpepsy/jsn097

6. Nickmilder M, Bernard A. Ecological association between childhood asthma and availability of indoor chlorinated swimming pools in Europe. *Occup Environ Med*. Jan 2007;64(1):37-46. doi:10.1136/oem.2005.025452

7. Bernard A, Carbonnelle S, Dumont X, Nickmilder M. Infant swimming practice, pulmonary epithelium integrity, and the risk of allergic and respiratory diseases later in childhood. *Pediatrics*. Jun 2007;119(6):1095-103. doi:10.1542/peds.2006-3333

8. Font-Ribera L, Villanueva CM, Nieuwenhuijsen MJ, Zock JP, Kogevinas M, Henderson J. Swimming pool attendance, asthma, allergies, and lung function in the Avon Longitudinal Study of Parents and Children cohort. *Am J Respir Crit Care Med*. Mar 1 2011;183(5):582-8. doi:10.1164/rccm.201005-0761OC

9. Parker HE, Blanksby BA. Starting age and aquatic skill learning in young children: mastery of prerequisite water confidence and basic aquatic locomotion skills. *Aust J Sci Med Sport*. Sep 1997;29(3):83-7.

10. ACFASP Scientific Review: Minimum Age for Swimming Lessons. *American Red Cross Advisory Council on First Aid, Aquatics, Safety, and Preparedness*. June 2009

11. Chandy D, Richards D. Drowning (submersion injuries). UpToDate. Updated July 8, 2024. Accessed August 27, 2024. https://www.uptodate.com/contents/drowning-submersion-injuries

12. Turgut A, Turgut T. A study on rescuer drowning and multiple drowning incidents. *J Safety Res*. Apr 2012;43(2):129-32. doi:10.1016/j.jsr.2012.05.001

13. Noonan L, Howrey R, Ginsburg CM. Freshwater submersion injuries in children: a retrospective review of seventy-five hospitalized patients. *Pediatrics*. Sep 1996;98(3 Pt 1):368-71.

14. Stern A, Thompson L. What Parents Should Know About Drowning and Dry Drowning. JAMA Pediatrics. Updated June 27, 2022. Accessed August 27, 2024. https://jamanetwork.com/journals/jamapediatrics/fullarticle/2793341

15. Tobin JM, Ramos WD, Greenshields J, et al. Outcome of Conventional Bystander Cardiopulmonary Resuscitation in Cardiac Arrest Following Drowning. *Prehosp Disaster Med*. Apr 2020;35(2):141-147. doi:10.1017/S1049023X20000060

16. Thompson DC, Rivara FP. Pool fencing for preventing drowning in children. *Cochrane Database Syst Rev*. 2000;1998(2):CD001047. doi:10.1002/14651858.CD001047

17. Safety Barrier Guidelines for Residential Pools. *US Consumer Product Safety Commission*. June 2012 Publication 362

Chapter 7

Other Vehicles

This chapter includes all-terrain vehicles (ATV)/4-wheelers, dirt bikes, bicycles, scooters, golf carts, snow skis, water skis, jet skis, snowmobiles, horses, and any other moving object. I have three suggestions here:

1. WEAR A HELMET
2. Review safety with your children prior to letting them on
3. Follow any rules by the manufacturer, such as age and weight limits

Helmet Use

Let's talk about helmets. They absolutely save lives, and they absolutely can prevent brain injury when worn correctly. A 2017 systematic review and meta-analysis (highest possible quality study type that summarizes multiple studies) showed that wearing a helmet while riding a bicycle reduced chances of head injury by more than 50%, serious head injury by 70%, face injury by 33%, and fatal head injury by 65%.[1] They may look dorky to some older children, and they might be uncomfortable, but you should make a point to make your child wear a helmet, period. This one simple rule can make a huge difference in your child's risk of major injury. Again, bones heal, but head injuries might not. Also, be aware that helmet use may not be optional in your state. Currently 21 states and the District of Columbia require children to wear bike helmets.

As far as appropriate helmets are concerned, recognize there are different helmets made for different activities. Bicycle helmets are different from baseball helmets, which are both different from ski helmets. Make sure the appropriate helmet is being worn for the appropriate activity. When purchasing a helmet, look for approval by the appropriate helmet credentialing body. Bicycle helmets, for example, are tested by the U.S. Consumer Product Safety Commission (CPSC) and should be certified. Baseball helmets are tested by the National Operating Committee on Standards for Athletic Equipment (NOCSAE). The CDC has a helpful website for helmet safety that has links to each type of potential helmet your child may need at https://www.cdc.gov/heads-up/safety/?CDC_AAref_Val=https://www.cdc.gov/headsup/helmets/index.html.[2]

When selecting the right size for your child, *Consumer Reports* suggests one of the best ways is to take your child to a bike shop and have them try on helmets with a professional.[3] However, many of us purchase products online or do not have a bike shop nearby. *Two Wheeling Tots* is an online bike review website that reviews multiple types of bikes, scooters, and helmets. They have an excellent guide online for sizing your helmet with 6 easy steps and pictures included[4], which can be found at: https://www.twowheelingtots.com/kids-bike-helmet-sizes-guide/. You should measure your child's head circumference one inch above their eyebrows and select a helmet that is within their head circumference range because bike helmets have adjustable circumferences. Their other recommended steps include:

- Remove any thick ponytails or hair clips that may prevent the helmet from sitting flush on a child's head
- Place the helmet squarely on top of your child's head, the helmet should sit about two finger widths above the child's eyebrows
- The child should be able to fit just one finger between their chin and the strap of the helmet.

Consumer Reports recommends based on an expert's opinion that you pull lightly on top of the helmet while strapped, the helmet should not come off of their head.[3] You should frequently check the child's bike helmet fitting and make appropriate adjustments as needed. Of note, one study found a nearly two-fold risk of head injury in children whose helmets did not fit properly during a bicycle crash.[5] Also, bike helmets do expire, so check your manufacturer instructions for the expiration date.

According to the American Academy of Orthopedic Surgeons (AAOS), in general, the helmet should be snug and not slide from side-to-side or front-to-back.[6] It should be level and cover the top of the forehead without tilting in any direction. It should be stable, meaning the chinstrap keeps the helmet from rocking in any direction. If a major fall occurs and the helmet suffers any damage, *replace it*. Do not ride a bike with a child under the age of one. These should be fairly easy rules to follow. Likewise, other activities such as horseback riding and ski sports are best done while wearing a helmet.

Similar to car seats, *Consumer Reports* publishes reviews on bicycle helmets every year. The CPSC has minimum requirements, but *Consumer Reports* tries to stratify helmet safety with multiple tests, including: dropping a weight from the buckled chin strap to check its strength and an impact test dropping the helmet 6.5 feet onto a steel anvil at 14 mph at multiple angles.[7] Their bike helmet crash testing website has fun videos of all the tests in motion. They also include special features, ease of use, and ventilation ratings.

The Dangers of Fast-Moving Toys

Of the entire list, ATVs scare me the most. I have seen severe traumas in children from ATVs, and there have been multiple deaths in children in my geographical territory over the years. During my training in the Trauma Intensive Care Unit (ICU), I saw a high school aged girl who was involved in an ATV crash and her head was injured. The parents had just been let back into the ICU to see their daughter on a ventilator. I watched a neurosurgery resident walk in and tell the mother that they had to take her daughter to the operating room immediately to drill holes in the skull to remove the pressure from the internal bleeding, using the words "this is her best chance for survival." I watched that poor mother stumble and have to be carried out of the ICU in tears, and it broke my heart. My wife and I had not yet had our first child, but I vowed in that moment to do my best to keep them from a similar tragedy. Fortunately, the girl survived but had traumatic brain damage.

When it comes to ATV popularity, one study showed an increase in ATV accidents of 240% between 1997 and 2006 and a 476% increase in spinal injury rate from ATV use.[8] Spine injuries in children are extremely rare from minor trauma, such as a ground level fall, and are usually an indicator of severe injury. The same can be said for fractures of the pelvis in children.

Going back to *Caveman Medicine*, people were not designed to be moving at fast speeds on a moving vehicle or to go down hills quickly with boards strapped to their feet as with ski sports. These are more modern inventions. With automobiles, the safety features keep up with the technology as best as they can. Automobiles are at least enclosed boxes with safety restraints and airbags. Cars have now been designed to collapse in such a way to absorb maximum impact. Newer vehicles even have safety features for collision avoidance, and some are even driving themselves now. Other moving vehicles like ATVs, UTVs, dirt bikes, etc. do not have the same amount of safety features. They are not designed with this in mind. Yes, a crash on the interstate in a car at 70 miles per hour is not a good thing, but a dirt bike crash at 15 miles per hour can be worse, even with a helmet. In my mind, these are more dangerous on a per use basis than riding in a car. Besides, riding in a car is essentially required to participate in life in the U.S. while riding an ATV is not for most people. I will never say never, but I do not plan on ever letting my children to drive or ride on one. ATVs are one of those things that make me super nervous. I've just seen too much. My official recommendation is to not let your children on an ATV or dirt bike. However, I do not judge anyone who allows their children to use them, I just reiterate again: make your child wear a helmet! You will never second guess the decision to make your child wear a helmet, even if they complain. You might, however, regret the decision not to enforce this rule. Likewise, I recommend you follow all applicable laws and manufacturer's guides for height, weight, driving ages, location for use, etc.

I know many people who let their children ride ATVs frequently. If you're going to let your child do it, make sure you review safety regularly with them. More children die each year on ATVs than in bicycle crashes, despite many more children riding bicycles than ATVs on a regular basis.[9] The following statistics have been pulled from the American Academy of Pediatrics (AAP) policy statement and review from 2022.[9] Major risk factors for ATV crashes resulting in death include:

- Age younger than 16 (interestingly this coincides with the age of independent driving in many states),
- Male (70% of all crash victims)
- ATV size (a child riding on an adult size vehicle),
- Riding on the roadway (greater than 50% of all pediatric fatalities),
- Carrying a passenger (most ATVs are made for a single rider)
- Lack of helmet use.

Especially as your children get older, I recommend discussing rules about what to do at other children's houses. Many accidents occur when a child who is unfamiliar with such motorized vehicles goes to someone else's house and rides on one. The visiting child is less likely to know the necessary safety measures or how to operate the vehicle. When your child is going somewhere without your supervision, remember to go over your household rules or to check with the adults supervising at the child's play destination.

I will reiterate the younger age and male aspects because this should make sense to you. Males, and typically younger males, are more likely to engage in riskier behaviors. In other words, boys are stupid when it comes to bodily harm. I thought I was invincible until about the age I got married. At that time, I became responsible to and for someone else besides my parents, and the anti-risk parts of my brain became more functional. Having children took that to an even greater level. If you want to know some truths about life, then look no further than the price of buying insurance. Males younger than 25 are typically charged higher rates (unless they get married) for car insurance. I have three sons, and my wife can attest how true this is, and they haven't even reached adolescence yet. My oldest is not scared of *anything*, and that's scary to us as his parents. Outdoor recreational vehicles can be a source of incredible fun and extremely helpful if you live on a large plot of land, but please pay attention to the risk factors above, and try to do anything you can to avoid these situations.

Lastly, I will note that younger ages are more dangerous likely because they do not have experience operating motor vehicles. Children 16 and older typically do have some experience and this likely contributes to slightly less risk of injury, but high school and even college aged young adults are at high risk of injury, particularly if alcohol is involved.

Bicycles

Bicycles are a normal part of life for many, and we are no exception in our household. Going back to my advice, we make our children wear helmets. All it takes is one quick accident and serious injury can occur, and it's preventable. Our biggest battle is making sure our children obey the rules about not going onto the road when an adult is not around. Many child deaths from bicycles occur from the child getting struck by a vehicle in the road. The road is a dangerous place. Keeping our checklist in mind, make sure your children know the rules about roads and enforce them. Some people live in rural areas where this may not be as much of a concern, others live in neighborhoods with little or no traffic, and some live in big cities with heavier traffic. Know your situation. Maybe you live in a smaller neighborhood, but you just moved in and you're the only household with small children. Maybe the other neighbors are not used to having to drive slowly near your house. It never hurts to stand in the road when your children are playing in the driveway and greet your new neighbors. They will be more likely to pay attention when driving near your house. If they don't, consider politely requesting they slow down near your house, especially if you catch their attention while they're driving by. Worst case scenario, call the local police and ask them to patrol your area if you're concerned. Yes, it's your responsibility to watch your children, but you're not perfect, and others have a responsibility as well, especially with regards to speed limits. It's your child's life we're talking about here; never be afraid to inconvenience people on behalf of your child's safety.

Bicycle crashes are the most common cause of head injuries in children.[10] Going beyond limb trauma that I treat regularly, head injuries are way more likely to cause permanent injury or death. A study of bicycle injuries in 1998 showed that approximately 84% of bicycle injuries that wind up in an emergency trauma center are most often caused by a crash with a motor vehicle.[11] Seventy-nine percent of injuries were males, and only 3 children of 211 studied (1.4%) were wearing helmets at the time of injury. Make your child wear a bicycle helmet, and maintain extreme caution with bicycles near any roads.

Scooters, Hoverboards, Skateboards, and Onewheels

When I was in residency, a middle-aged man came into our hospital with a tibia fracture from falling off a hoverboard. It was a day or two before Christmas, and he had purchased it for his adolescent daughter and wanted to try it out before Christmas day prior to giving it to his daughter. Instead, he had surgery the day before Christmas and reportedly returned the hoverboard to the store. I'm sure there are many other similar stories out there, but the rise of hoverboards and Onewheels (motorized skateboards with one central wheel) certainly has led to more broken bones in the recent years. Scooters and skateboards have been around longer, and they still are a common cause of broken bones. Just as with bicycles, you should make your child wear a helmet when using any of these devices. Broken bones are very treatable, but head injuries can potentially be serious.

As an orthopedist, the most common injuries I see from this category as well as bicycles are fractured wrists and forearms. In fact, I once treated both of my good friends' children within 8 weeks of one another. Both of their children broke their wrists on the same Onewheel, and the parents got rid of it afterward. Though you see an occasional severe fracture that requires surgery, typically these injuries will not cause any long-term disability. Though unlikely to kill your child, the potential is there if they are not wearing a helmet. Additionally, as an orthopedist, I highly endorse wrist guards, elbow pads, and knee pads for your child unless you enjoy spending more time at the doctor's office!

Golf Carts

Golf carts are an under appreciated risk for injury in general. They have become more popular around neighborhoods and for recreational use outside of the golf course over the past decade or so. Golf carts can have seatbelts installed, but they have open sides and lack airbags, despite some of them easily reaching and sometimes exceeding 25 mile per hour speeds. Typically, crashes happen as rollovers because they are top heavy, and people sometimes forget how dangerous they can be if not driven carefully. This is not a common source of death in and of itself, but it is best to make sure your child is appropriately seated and understands the rules of being on a golf cart when riding. If you are going to allow your child to drive, it is important to teach them about the dangers of golf carts and particularly the potential to flip the golf cart when making turns. In one city that I worked in, I knew of a few high school students who ended up in an ICU from taking a sharp turn down a hill in a golf cart. Serious injuries can and do occur. I personally think golf carts are a wonderful option for fun in the neighborhood, and they've certainly been a part of our children's lives because their grandparents own one and take them on routine trips around their neighborhood. Regardless, you should review your state laws and manufacturer guidelines to check prior to letting your child ride or drive on one.

Water Skiing, Jet Skis, and Boats

Deaths due to watercraft in children are a rare event, but they still happen. Data is available through the CDC Wide-ranging Online Data for Epidemiologic Research (WONDER) Database. From 2018 through 2021, there were 25 deaths in ages 5-9, 35 in ages 10-14, and 81 in ages 15-19.[12] This averages to 6.25 deaths per year, 8.75 deaths per year, and 20.25 deaths per year, respectively. Data includes deaths on motorized vehicles, such as fishing boats, ferries, and jet skis as well as non-motorized vehicles, such as kayaks, canoes, and surfboards. Deaths were caused by either drowning or direct injury. Taking this into account, this is fortunately a rare event, but major injuries can still happen. Limb trauma can still be significant.

Comparing small boats and jet skis, one review found that children injured in jet ski accidents compared with small boat accidents were more likely to require surgery as well as suffer closed-head injuries, spinal injuries, and death.[13] Faster moving objects tend to create a higher risk of worse injuries in general. If you're going to let your children ride motorized water vehicles, you should always make them wear a US Coast Guard approved life jacket and be cautious when letting them drive. Be sure to obey all your state laws with respect to appropriate ages for riding and/or driving the vehicle.

Ski Sports

Snow skiing and snowboarding are fun sports, but not everyone does them. For some, it's a regular part of life due to living in geographical proximity to a ski area. Pediatric limb trauma rarely requires surgery in many parts of the country. The riskiest activities seem to be monkey bars, sports, and bicycles in my territory. However, major surgery is rarely necessary for these injuries in children (unlike adults, when surgery is necessary more often than not due to the reduced amount of bone remodeling potential). In trauma centers in areas like Colorado, for instance, surgical necessity is much more common in the pediatric population because of skiing. It turns out that one of the most dangerous things for a child's limb is to secure it to some sort of stiff boot and a piece of wood and send them down a hill at high speeds. While an ankle sprain during a soccer game can be painful, running on grass is not a very risky activity for serious injury. I plan on taking our children skiing one day, and I personally think it's a highly enjoyable activity when I get the rare chance. If you take your children skiing, make sure to do ski school with them, and be cautious about letting them go somewhere without adult supervision. And, of course, wear a helmet. One study found rates of traumatic brain injury were lessened by 35% with helmet use and other head injuries (face, etc.) were lessened by 58% with ski injuries.[14] Helmet use is one of those rules you should enforce as a parent.

If you're curious as to which is more dangerous between snowboarding and skiing, one study found the following: skiers had higher injury severity scores on average.[15] While head, abdominal, and upper extremity injuries were slightly more frequent in snowboarders, skiers were more likely to sustain face, chest, and lower extremity injuries. Skiers were more likely to undergo surgery, but the need for intensive care and mortality were no different between the two. What's my take? They're equally dangerous and I don't think it matters which your child picks from a purely safety standpoint.

Summary

To summarize, wear a helmet, wear a helmet, WEAR A HELMET! It's not hard to do, it's not a big deal, and it's worth the fight to engrain that in your child's head. It's similar to wearing a seatbelt in a car. You just do it and make it a habit for your children. I am not going to advocate for you making your child sit in bubble wrap and never risking injury. On the contrary, I know very well how good children are at healing themselves from injury. They're made to recover from injury. If they're like mine, they seem hellbent on getting injured. But the injuries that are sustained from moving devices as mentioned in this chapter are relatively newer in human history, and we aren't made to heal from some of those injuries. If you ask anyone who knows me, I'm a very laid-back person. I don't stress about my kids getting hurt in most situations because I know it's a part of life. But there are some things that my medical experience has taught me that I won't let my children do. Maybe I'm a little overly cautious with ATVs and dirt bikes (my wife occasionally rode them growing up), but if you're going to let your child do it, know the risks and frequently review safety with your child. Know your child and know their limits. No child is capable of consistently making good, rational decisions for themselves, but some certainly seem better about not engaging in dangerous activities than others. My children are certainly on the riskier side of the spectrum, so my trust level with them is lower for fast-moving objects.

***

References

1. Olivier J, Creighton P. Bicycle injuries and helmet use: a systematic review and meta-analysis. *Int J Epidemiol*. Feb 1 2017;46(1):278-292. doi:10.1093/ije/dyw153

2. Safety Guidelines: Helmets. Center for Disease Control: Heads Up. Updated April 5, 2024. Accessed August 27, 2024. https://www.cdc.gov/heads-up/safety/?CDC_AAref_Val=https://www.cdc.gov/headsup/helmets/index.html

3. Abramson A. How to Choose a Bike Helmet for a Child. Consumer Reports. Updated March 29, 2024. Accessed August 27, 2024. https://www.consumerreports.org/health/bike-helmets/how-to-choose-a-bike-helmet-for-a-child-a6923950811/

4. Wren C. Kids Bike Helmet Sizes and Fit Guide. Two Wheeling Tots. Updated September 27, 2023. Accessed August 27, 2024. https://www.twowheelingtots.com/kids-bike-helmet-sizes-guide/

5. Rivara FP, Astley SJ, Clarren SK, Thompson DC, Thompson RS. Fit of bicycle safety helmets and risk of head injuries in children. *Inj Prev*. Sep 1999;5(3):194-7. doi:10.1136/ip.5.3.194

6. Witstein J. Helmet Safety. OrthoInfo by AAOS. Updated August 2022. Accessed August 27, 2024. https://orthoinfo.aaos.org/en/staying-healthy/helmet-safety#:~:text=Wearing%20a%20bike%20helmet%20while%20rid-

ing%20a%20bicycle,matter%20how%20short.%20Many%20accidents%20happen%20near%20home.

7. Santanachote P. What Happens When Consumer Reports Tests Bike Helmets. Consumer Reports. Updated August 31, 2021. Accessed August 27, 2024. https://www.consumerreports.org/bike-helmets/what-happens-when-consumer-reports-tests-bike-helmets-a1276696221/

8. Sawyer JR, Bernard MS, Schroeder RJ, Kelly DM, Warnersurname WC, Jr. Trends in all-terrain vehicle-related spinal injuries in children and adolescents. *J Pediatr Orthop*. Sep 2011;31(6):623-7. doi:10.1097/BPO.ob013e31822a2f0f

9. Jennissen CA, Denning GM, Aitken ME, et al. American Academy of Pediatrics Recommendations for the Prevention of Pediatric ATV-Related Deaths and Injuries. *Pediatrics*. Oct 1 2022;150(4)doi:10.1542/peds.2022-059279

10. Weiss BD. Bicycle-related head injuries. *Clin Sports Med*. Jan 1994;13(1):99-112.

11. Puranik S, Long J, Coffman S. Profile of pediatric bicycle injuries. *South Med J*. Nov 1998;91(11):1033-7. doi:10.1097/00007611-199811000-00008

12. Data from: Centers for Disease Control and Prevention, National Center for Health Statistics. National Vital Statistics System, Mortality 2018-2022 on CDC WONDER Online Database, released in 2024. Data are from the Multiple Cause of Death Files, 2018-2022, as compiled from data provided by the 57 vital statistics jurisdictions through the Vital Statistics Cooperative Program. Accessed at http://wonder.cdc.gov/ucd-icd10-expanded.html on Aug 27, 2024.

13. Beierle EA, Chen MK, Langham MR, Jr., Kays DW, Talbert JL. Small watercraft injuries in children. *Am Surg*. Jun 2002;68(6):535-8; discussion 538.

14. Bailly N, Laporte JD, Afquir S, et al. Effect of Helmet Use on Traumatic Brain Injuries and Other Head Injuries in Alpine Sport.

Wilderness Environ Med. Jun 2018;29(2):151-158. doi:10.1016/j.wem.2017.11.007

15. Polites SF, Mao SA, Glasgow AE, Moir CR, Habermann EB. Safety on the slopes: ski versus snowboard injuries in children treated at United States trauma centers. *J Pediatr Surg.* May 2018;53(5):1024-1027. doi:10.1016/j.jpedsurg.2018.02.044

Chapter 8

Falls

According to WISQARS, the leading cause of *nonfatal* injury in children under age 14 is an unintentional fall. I recounted earlier in this book about one of our personal experiences with our oldest son falling down a set of stairs. This happened at an unfamiliar location without protection, so we had to be more cautious. Even though I was very careful about watching the stairwell, a split-second lapse led to my son falling down the stairs. He was fine, but it certainly scared us. Unintentional falls are responsible for many visits to the Emergency Department (ED). In 2019, there were 106,960 ED visits for age less than one, 584,584 visits in ages 1 to 4, 436,858 for 5 to 9, and 384,775 for ages 10-19. That's over 1,000,000 visits to the ED for unintentional falls in a single year. Most of these thankfully do not result in severe injury, but it is certainly an alarming event.

The checklist to preventing falls:

1. Gates on stairways in your house
2. No baby walkers upstairs, or at least constant monitoring
3. Keep windows locked and secured

Many new parents, me included, imagine the first 6 months to be the toughest part of the first few years of parenting when they have not yet experienced it. Everyone's main concern is the baby sleeping. However, my wife and I realized how much more stressful life is after that 6-month time period by the time we had our second. The reality is that infants who are less than 6 months old are very easy to watch despite crying fits and sleeping troubles because they physically cannot move themselves. If you leave them lying on the floor for a minute to go pour a cup of coffee, they will be right there when you get back. Once they start crawling and, in particular walking, that's when it gets harder to watch a child. It changes drastically because they can move. And when you have more than one child, you end up watching the younger one more closely, and the oldest can find more ways to sneak off and get injured.

Just like any other section we've covered, the best thing you can do is create safety guards to reduce the chances of serious injury. Place gates on all stairways. It's relatively inexpensive and simple to do. Make sure they are always closed. If you have riskier furniture with sharp edges, it is probably best to move them away from areas where your children play a lot or to purchase edge covers to line your sharper table edges. If you already have children, you know they're basically dangerous clumsy monkeys that treat everything in your house like a playground. They will also do the same at other locations, so make sure to take precautions, including possibly purchasing stair gates for the grandparents' houses or other caretakers. Also, be aware of anything they can climb on, such as bookshelves that can tip over. Install anti-tip brackets behind bookshelves.

One review tells us that the mortality rate is one percent for falls less than 15 feet.[1] That's a fairly large distance to fall if you think about it: one and a half basketball hoops tall. The rate climbs to 2.4% for falls over 15 feet. To say this another way: 97.6% of falls *over 15 feet* do not result in death. That includes falls from second story windows. Though this should not be ignored as a major risk for health, it should bring some comfort that the *vast majority* of falls do not result in death. One study found the average fall height that resulted in death is between five and six stories (50 to 60 feet high)[2] whereas another study concludes that falls of less than 10 feet are not likely to cause serious injury.[3] The most common non-head injuries were upper extremity fracture at 6.2% and lower extremity fracture at 5.6%, which are fixable problems. All told, this should bring you comfort, especially if you do not live on a higher story of an apartment building. While falls are dangerous, there are more common sources of death in children, especially when taking into consideration how often children fall off objects.

Going back to *Caveman Medicine*, children have been falling from heights throughout our history as human beings, so their bodies are more adept at surviving and healing compared to something like a high-speed car wreck. This is true for at least lower heights, such as 10 feet or less. Children probably constantly fell from tall rocks or trees as we progressed toward civilization.

Windows

Windows are a source of potential falls. Approximately eight children less than age five die from falls from windows every year, essentially all from the second story or higher.[4] Approximately 3,300 children visit the ED each year for falls from windows, of which 45% sustain serious injuries including head injury and fracture.[5] Likewise, children that live in apartment buildings are up to five times more likely to fall from a window compared to children that live in a house. If you do live in an apartment on a higher floor or if you have a two or more-story house, you should buy child safety locks for windows, which are relatively inexpensive and may make a big difference. Likewise, do not put furniture near windows if you can avoid it, especially at a high-risk window. The American Academy of Pediatrics in their policy statement report windows should not open more than 4 inches for child safety.[2] Building codes typically follow this by requiring railing on balconies to have no more than 4-inch width on the vertical bars. Reportedly, no child over the age of one can fit their head through a gap this size. Some window locks prevent windows from opening more than 4 inches, so they may be worth purchasing.

Infant Walkers

Infant walkers are another potential danger.[4] Approximately 230,676 children less than 15 months of age were treated between 1990 and 2014 for infant-walker related injuries with the median age being 8.2 months, which averages to 9,612 per year.[6] Approximately 74% of the injuries came from a fall down multiple stairs while 15% came from the child falling out of the walker itself. Others were treated for burns or other hazards because the walker provides access to areas that the child might not have been otherwise able to reach, such as the stove. This study includes some years after 2008, when the latest safety standards were updated by the Consumer Product Safety Improvement Act of 2008.[7] Be careful with infant walkers if you are going to use them. Make sure the areas in which you are using them are set up for safety. My personal advice is not to use them. Children are much easier to watch when they can't leave the spot in which you place them anyway. Stationary play stations and play pens are better.

Shopping Carts and Truck Beds

Other areas to be cautious include shopping cart falls or spills, which are responsible for 24,100 ED visits per year in children under age 15, as well as pickup truck cargo areas.[8] Kids should always be seated in a shopping cart and secured with the strap that comes with the cart. They should never be standing. The backs of pick-up trucks are not safe for riding and were reported to the source of approximately 200 deaths per year in a study from the year 2000, with half of the deaths occurring in children.[9] In some states, riding in the back of a pickup truck is illegal. The fall injury category in many databases does include falls from bicycles, skating, scooters, and skateboarding among others. As I stated in an earlier chapter, children should wear a helmet when participating in these activities. Period.

* * *

References

1.Wang MY, Kim KA, Griffith PM, et al. Injuries from falls in the pediatric population: an analysis of 729 cases. *J Pediatr Surg*. Oct 2001;36(10):1528-34. doi:10.1053/jpsu.2001.27037

2.Committee on I, Poison P. American Academy of Pediatrics: Falls from heights: windows, roofs, and balconies. *Pediatrics*. May 2001;107(5):1188-91. doi:10.1542/peds.107.5.1188

3.Williams RA. Injuries in infants and small children resulting from witnessed and corroborated free falls. *J Trauma*. Oct 1991;31(10):1350-2. doi:10.1097/00005373-199110000-00005

4.Gill A, Kelly N. Prevention of falls and fall-related injuries in children. UpToDate. Updated July 2024. Accessed August 27, 2024. https://www.uptodate.com/contents/prevention-of-falls-and-fall-related-injuries-in-children?search=trampoline&source=search_result&

selectedTitle=1~13&usage_type=default&display_rank=1#H29

5.CPSC: Parents, Caregivers Should Consider Safety Before Opening Windows. U.S. Consumer Product Safety Commission. Updated April 8, 2011. Accessed 2024, August 27. https://www.cpsc.gov/Newsroom/News-Releases/2011/CPSC-Parents-Caregivers-Should-Consider-Safety-Before-Opening-Windows

6.Sims A, Chounthirath T, Yang J, Hodges NL, Smith GA. Infant Walker-Related Injuries in the United States. *Pediatrics*. Oct 2018;142(4)doi:10.1542/peds.2017-4332

7.The Consumer Product Safety Improvement Act. U.S. Consumer Product Safety Commission. Accessed August 27, 2024.

https://www.cpsc.gov/Regulations-Laws--Standards/Statutes/The-Consumer-Product-Safety-Improvement-Act

8.Martin KJ, Chounthirath T, Xiang H, Smith GA. Pediatric shopping-cart-related injuries treated in US emergency departments, 1990-2011. *Clin Pediatr (Phila)*. Mar 2014;53(3):277-85. doi:10.1177/0009922813513322

9.Christoffel T, Agran P, Winn D, Anderson C, Del Valle C. Developing a model law restricting the transporting of passengers in the cargo areas of pickup trucks. *J Public Health Policy*. 2000;21(1):61-81.

Chapter 9
Trampolines and Playgrounds

When I was a child, we had a trampoline and a playground at our house. Our trampoline did not have a circumferential safety net as is standard nowadays. My sisters and I fortunately never sustained major injuries, but we had a lot of fun. I used to love the Disney cartoon version of *Peter Pan*. My mother sewed me a costume when I was around the age of 5, and I wore it around the house and yard frequently. One time, I decided to pretend to be Peter Pan fighting Captain Hook on his pirate ship, and I wanted to cut through a sail like Peter Pan does in the film. I took the largest bread knife we had from the kitchen and stabbed through the middle of our trampoline, just like the movie. I fell through the middle, and I don't think my parents were very happy about having to patch a giant hole in the trampoline jumping pad. It's funny the memories we carry with us vividly through life. My story also illustrates the silly logic of children, but the potentially stupid and dangerous things they can do. Needless to say, I am much more responsible with knives as a surgeon than I was as a child!

Because I had a trampoline growing up and have fond memories, I own a trampoline. I also own a playground for my children. They are great sources of entertainment for children, and though they carry danger, you do the best you can to keep children safe by taking precautions while still letting them have fun and grow. The American Academy of Pediatrics (AAP) discourages home use of trampolines, so I guess I'm a bad parent, but I grew up with a trampoline and I loved it. Though people can die on trampolines and many people sustain injuries, they can be fun, just like bicycles.

Trampolines

Trampoline Safety Checklist:

1. Has a safety net
2. Dug into the ground so it's at ground level if possible
3. Appropriate padding covering the springs
4. Make sure the trampoline is on flat ground and not an incline or hill
5. Do not let your children crawl under the trampoline
6. Always supervise

For trampolines, make sure you purchase one with a safety net. In fact, I do not believe they even sell trampolines without them anymore. Some companies make trampolines that are level with the ground to take the height out of potential falls that could occur outside of the net. Make sure your children are opening and shutting the zipper door appropriately when entering and exiting the trampoline. We remind our children of this rule consistently, so they know it is a routine part of playing on the trampoline. Trampolines have the added risk of a child catching their leg or arm between the springs, so periodically check that your pad is in good shape and replace it if needed. Most sources also recommend not letting more than one child on the trampoline at one time, but I confess that I break this recommendation routinely. I even broke my son's foot by bouncing with him on the trampoline.

A study in a medical journal called *Pediatric Emergency Care* reported approximately 800,000 children were treated for trampoline injuries from 2009-2018, or 80,000 per year.[1] Surprisingly, no deaths were reported during this time frame, and in keeping with the theme of this book, that's the most important finding in my opinion. Thirty four percent were treated for fractures, 33% for sprains, and 14% for bruises and scrapes. Also, adolescents were more at risk of limb injury and concussion than toddlers and children ages 2-12.

Trampoline Parks

Trampoline parks are increasing in popularity, and the first time I went to one, it struck me how odd it was to sign such an aggressive waiver to enter the park. I will say that some of the worst limb injuries I've seen in children have come from trampoline parks occasionally, and usually adolescents are the ones that get hurt rather than smaller children. One patient even had their ankle ripped open and turned backward at one park. I still let my children go to trampoline parks, but I make sure to watch them carefully and enforce the rules. I'm more worried about flips and landing on a neck than I am a limb, and if I ever notice my children acting carelessly, I pull them off immediately.

Inflatable Bounce Devices

Inflatable bounce houses can be just as risky as trampolines, so always monitor your child when they are using one. There are many great options for purchase for home use that many of our relatives and friends have. If you purchase one, make sure to read all the instructions and weigh it down appropriately per the manufacturer guidelines, most often with anchors of some sort. You should periodically inspect for any holes or damage, and you should replace it every few years. Expiration dates are often available in the manufacturer's handbook or their website.

Playgrounds

We purchased a playground for our back yard, and our kids love it. Playgrounds are a great source of fun for children and encourage them to play outside. Here are the safety tips for playground use, especially if installing one at your house:

1. Make sure the playground is age appropriate
2. Use soft material below the playground like mulch or rubber playground materials
3. Supervise

Here are some sobering statistics on playgrounds. From 1990 to 2000, 147 children died from playground injury, 82 of which were strangulations and 31 were falls.[2] That means most playground deaths occur from the child accidentally strangulating themselves in the equipment rather than falling, and most of these deaths occurred on home playgrounds. If you break this down, that is approximately 14-15 deaths per year during that time period. However, to put this in perspective, think of how many children play on playgrounds nearly daily at school or otherwise. Certainly, deaths can happen, but for the most part playgrounds are a ubiquitous part of childhood play, and I definitely would not advocate to keep your child from ever playing on one. Instead, make sure you supervise your child and stick to age recommendations on playgrounds. They are designed and designated that way for a reason.

Falls are the leading cause of injury from playgrounds, and the most severe injuries are typically fractures (I would never have guessed!). Arm fractures are the most common injury I treat, and most of the time it is either a sport or a playground injury. In fact, playgrounds are responsible for the most injuries that require surgical treatment in children in my practice, mostly the elbow. Despite this, I still let my children play on playgrounds and even own one. Most children sustain injuries when they intentionally try to jump from a swing or a high area. Monkey bars are one of the biggest offenders. Rates of injury increase as the equipment exceeds 5 to 6 feet in height, so consider this when installing your own playground. The Consumer Product Safety Commission (CPSC) recommends using mulch, fine sand, or shredded rubber as the base for the playground as well as maintaining a depth of 12 inches and 6 feet of border in all directions around equipment.[3] In some studies, sand has been shown to be better than grass while wood chips or synthetic rubber chips are the best for preventing injury by way of energy absorption at impact.[4] We have mulch around ours.

Playground Material Toxicitiy

There is an ongoing debate on the potential toxicity of rubber playground materials, typically made from recycled tire waste. At the current time, there are no studies that support that exposure to these materials increases risks of cancer or other medical issues, but it is difficult to monitor this type of data over a long period of time. The concern comes from the fact that these artificial playground materials contain small amounts of various chemicals that have the potential to cause adverse health effects.[5] Various small exposures to the skin are unlikely to cause problems, but there is a theoretical risk with a large amount of exposures over time. The CPSC acknowledges that "no specific chemical hazards from recycled tires in playground surfacing are known by the CPCS at this time" but also recommends the following precautions to limit exposure[6]:

- Avoid mouth contact with playground surfacing materials because this may pose a choking hazard regardless of chemical exposure,
- Avoid eating food or drinking beverages while directly on playground surfaces, and wash hands before handling food
- Limit the time at a playground on extremely hot days

- Clean hands and other areas of exposed skin after visiting the playground, and consider changing clothes if evidence of tire materials (e.g., black marks or dust) is visible on fabrics,
- Clean any toys that were used on a playground after the visit.

If you are at all concerned, use natural materials on your own home playground if you have one, such as mulch.

Summary

Trampolines and playgrounds have their risks, but these do not worry me as much as other activities that my children could do. If you choose to let your children play on trampolines, I recommend you follow the checklist I have provided with the understanding that injuries will likely happen regardless. Thankfully these are rarely fatal. Similar to pools, be aware that you could be liable for injuries that occur on your playground if they are not properly secured.

* * *

References

1. Hussein MH, Toreih AA, Attia AS, et al. Trampoline Injuries in Children and Adolescents: A Jumping Threat. *Pediatr Emerg Care*. Feb 1 2022;38(2):e894-e899. doi:10.1097/PEC.0000000000002457
2. Playground Safety Guide. OrthoInfo by AAOS. Updated April 2022. Accessed August 27, 2024. https://orthoinfo.aaos.org/en/staying-healthy/playground-safety-guide
3. Public Playground Safety Handbook. U.S. Consumer Product Safety Commission. Updated December 29, 2015. https://www.cpsc.gov/s3fs-public/325.pdf

4. Gill A, Kelly N. Prevention of falls and fall-related injuries in children. UpToDate. Updated July 2024. Accessed August 27, 2024. https://www.uptodate.com/contents/prevention-of-falls-and-fall-related-injuries-in-children?search=trampoline&source=search_result&selectedTitle=1~13&usage_type=default&display_rank=1#H29

5. Booker N, Fox-Rawlings S. Children and Athletes at Play on Toxic Turf and Playgrounds. Cancer Prevention & Treatment Fund. Accessed August 27, 2024. https://stopcancerfund.org/pz-environmental-exposures/caution-children-at-play-on-potentially-toxic-surfaces/

6. Status of CPSC's Review of Playgrounds with Crumb Rubber. U.S. Consumer Product Safety Commission. Accessed August 27, 2024. https://www.cpsc.gov/Safety-Education/Safety-Education-Centers/Crumb-Rubber-Safety-Information-Center

Chapter 10

Choking

Suffocation, or death by choking, is the 2nd leading cause of death in children under the age of 1, the 4th leading cause of accidental or traumatic death in children ages 1-4, and the 5th leading in children ages 5-9. I believe most parents are aware this is a danger. The biggest tip right off the bat is:

LEARN CPR AND THE HEIMLICH MANEUVER

Go to a CPR class. Get certified. It is rare you would ever need to do CPR on a child, but it never hurts to know the skill just in case. Basic Life Support (BLS) training provides the basics on what to do in emergency situations – recognizing when assistance is needed and the appropriate steps to take until help arrives.

The most important topic they cover for young parents is the Heimlich maneuver and how to perform it depending on the age of the child. Most of us have heard of the Heimlich and may have seen it portrayed in a show or movie but may not know how to actually perform the maneuver. The Heimlich maneuver is a first-aid procedure involving thrusts to the abdomen to remove airway blockages from objects such as toys or food. CPR is used to provide artificial ventilation, or breathing, and heart beats until help arrives. It is much more likely you would find yourself in a situation involving choking and needing to do the Heimlich maneuver. A BLS class will also teach you how to recognize signs of choking. Any person in a caregiver role with children should be familiar with BLS techniques and encouraged to also take a course. (see chapter 6 on drowning for reference to find classes).

Checklist for responding to choking:

1. Learn CPR and the Heimlich Maneuver
2. Prevent by sticking to appropriate foods for your child's age
3. Prevent by carefully monitoring for toys that are choking hazards

What is Choking?

What exactly is choking and how does it happen? Choking is the blockage of the airway, partially or completely. The back of your throat serves two major purposes, to pass food down into your stomach and to get air into your lungs. There is a junction at the back of the throat between the esophagus (the swallowing tube) and the trachea (the breathing tube). This entrance is usually open to both unless you are actively swallowing.

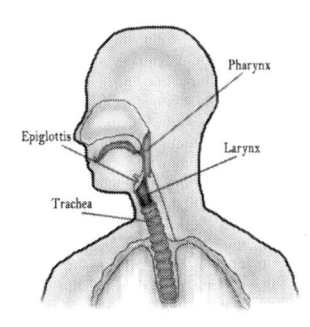

Image credit Persion Poet gal at English Wikipedia under the license Creative Commons Attribution-Share Alike 3.0 Unported, Image link: https://commons.wikimedia.org/wiki/File: Throat_Diagram.png , license link: https://creativecommons.org/ licenses/by-sa/3.0/

There is a piece of tissue called the epiglottis that acts as a flap to cover the trachea. When you swallow, the epiglottis is pushed down over the entrance to the trachea which forces food into the esophagus and keeps it from going into your lungs. This mechanism is not completely perfect, which is why people choke. If a piece of food or liquid gets too close to the entrance to the trachea, your body does an automatic cough and/or gag reflex in order to rid yourself of the obstruction.

Coughing and *gagging* are technically two different reflexes but often happen together. *Gagging* is the initial response in which the muscles of the throat constrict and may even lead to a vomiting episode as a response to large objects covering the throat. It is more sensitive and active in infants less than six months of age and diminishes from that point on as the infant begins to tolerate solid foods.[1] This is usually followed by coughing, which occurs when particles actually reach the opening to the airway or even get into the airway itself. Coughing involves the breathing muscles acting as a forceful push of air from the lungs to eject particles.

These reflexes are built-in for a reason, and they have saved all our lives multiple times. If you did not have a gag or cough reflex, you probably would've choked to death a hundred times already. Just as

God (or evolution if you prefer) knew young children were going to get hurt and needed a robust bone healing response, He knew we were going need a good mechanism to prevent choking from happening. I bring this up to note you should *not* interrupt anyone who is coughing or gagging and try to intervene. Let them try to cough it up themselves first. If the child is past the initial gag but is not coughing, or the cough is very weak, then it's time to intervene. Children are at higher risk of choking compared to adults because of the smaller diameter of the airway, meaning smaller objects can obstruct, and they have weaker cough muscles than adults.

My children have all choked on food at some point. At first, they stop eating and begin to gag, and my wife goes into a panic every time it happens. The vast majority of the time your child will be able to clear their own throat if you give them a chance. Taking that moment to let them cough can feel very long. If they have too much food in their mouth, carefully use your finger to sweep some out cautiously to avoid accidentally pushing food further in. Do not do sweeping maneuvers blindly, but only if you see a specific object causing the blockage. To reiterate, *do not* put your finger in a child's mouth if you cannot see the actual object; you could make the situation worse. If your child is actively gagging and/or coughing, they are trying to clear the problem themselves. It's the best mechanism, so do not interrupt. If they are coughing, it means they are still pushing air and that the airway is not completely blocked. If it were completely blocked, the child could not cough. The best thing to do is stand and monitor your child until they clear the blockage on their own. If they stop breathing and coughing completely or have a very weak cough, that's when it becomes serious, and the infant or toddler Heimlich maneuver may be required. Commonly recognized signs of choking include[2]:

- Gasping or wheezing
- Inability to talk or make a noise
- Turning blue in the face

- Grabbing their throat or waving the arms in the air
- Seeming panicked

Take note that choking may be silent, particularly in a small child who cannot come find you if distressed. Remain attentive in situations like eating and playing with unknown or small toys. If you recognize these signs in a child, call for help as you begin doing a series of chest blows and back blows. If you are by yourself, call 911 as your first step, then proceed to the maneuver as you're on speakerphone. Yell for help if it is available so they can call 911 while you are observing the child. You may be able to remove the obstruction with the maneuver quickly. It is common for the foreign body to be expelled forcefully or for vomiting to occur after performing the Heimlich maneuver successfully.

Periodically review how to do the Heimlich maneuver so you feel prepared if needed. You may attempt to sweep the throat if you can see the actual obstruction but do not try this if you cannot see it. For more information, see this website: https://advancedmedicalcertification.com/lesson/choking-treatment-adults-children-infants-bls-online-course-2020-2025/.

Newer Choking Rescue Devices

To aid in choking situations, there are some newer choking rescue devices available. One of the higher rated ones is called *LifeVac* and is available through major market retailers, such as Amazon. Another one is called *Dechoker*. These devices have a mask that fits over the mouth and nose and can be used on both children and adults. They involve a plunger type mechanism to create an airtight vacuum and suction objects out of the mouth. I have no actual experience with these devices, however the *Dechoker* is more invasive than *LifeVac* because it uses a tube that pushes into the oral cavity whereas the *LifeVac* does not. The Food and Drug Administration (FDA) has also evaluated the *Dechoker* because of a string of failures.[3]

These devices have been featured in some recent medical journal publications. One study tested both devices in fresh cadavers (dead bodies) with saltines, grapes, and cashews.[4] They found that the *Dechoker* was more likely to injure the tongue and failed to remove any of the obstructions. The *LifeVac* was able to remove the saltines but not the grapes or the cashews.

Another study compared abdominal thrusts (i.e. Heimlich maneuver) to both devices in manikins and found the *LifeVac* to be significantly more effective than abdominal thrusts (47 times as likely!) whereas the *Dechoker* was not found to be more effective.[5]

A third study evaluated real world use between 2016 and 2021 based on reports to device manufacturers.[6] They found choking symptoms were relieved in 123 of 124 cases with *LifeVac* and 60 of 61 cases with *Dechoker*. Adverse events reported included a case of lip laceration and a tooth injury with *Dechoker* as well as a case of the mask disconnecting from the bellows in the *LifeVac*. Abdominal thrusts and back blows were used as co-interventions in up to 39.5% of cases with *LifeVac* and up to 41% of cases with *Dechoker*.

A newer study reviewed cases from 2021 to 2023 and provided a questionnaire to the users, mostly family or friends of the victim.[7] *LifeVac* was successful in 151 of 157 cases in removing the obstruction and *Dechoker* was successful in 27 of 29. These cases were specifically noted to have the device be the last intervention used prior to relief of the obstruction. Other basic life support interventions, such as abdominal thrusts and chest blows, were used in 119 cases before the *LifeVac* was used. Adverse events included bruising around the mouth in two *LifeVac* cases while another 7 other adverse events could not be determined whether it was the fault of the *LifeVac* device or the foreign body itself.

What's my take on all this? Studies are promising and there are many testimonials of success from the users of these devices. I think they are both potentially good options for choking treatments and may do better than traditional abdominal thrusts for non-trained persons with little medical experience. If you choose to purchase one,

I recommend you still attend a CPR/BLS class because often classic BLS (CPR or Heimlich) maneuvers are required in real world events to assist with these devices, and the device must be available when needed. Formal studies are difficult to design for these types of devices, and more good quality research is required before I could recommend these as a "must have" type of device. Therefore, as a medical doctor I cannot specifically recommend for or against these devices, specifically compared to traditional life support maneuvers. When choosing between the two, *LifeVac* seems to have more cases studied and is non-invasive compared to *Dechoker*. Again, I have no real-world experience with these devices and cannot speak to how easy either of them is to use.

Prevention

As with many of these topics, the best way to treat the issue is prevention. Recognize what could be potential choking hazards to your child and remove access. In children ages 1 to 4 in 2019, there were 139 deaths due to suffocation. The WISQARS database reports approximately 25% of these were due to food and 20.9% were due to non-food items. Of note, 24.5% were due to accidental suffocation and strangulation in bed, such as younger children getting trapped underneath a pillow or loose sheet. With non-food items, place them up high, keep them locked up. This includes objects such as: toys with small parts, coins, buttons, balloons, pen caps, button batteries, and dog or cat food. There are many available cheap options to lock cabinets and drawers, but removing access with height and distance is safer.

Food items are so tempting to kids, and they don't realize the potential harm when it tastes so good! Pantries and other food storage should not be accessible to a small child who could get into risky foods. Each age will have appropriate foods based on size and texture. Commonly recognized foods to keep away from the reach of children include: grapes, berries, hotdogs, hard candy, popcorn, and chewing gum among others. There are multiple good resources for appropriate foods, including the CDC webpage[8] as well as healthychildren.org.[9]

One of the more difficult situations to control is having multiple children at different ages eating at the same time. For instance, if your older child is eating a hot dog, leaves their seat and your toddler can still reach the older child's leftovers, there is risk. Keeping track of toys is even more difficult than food. Toys for older children, like Legos® or marbles, can be dangerous to younger children. The multiple small pieces can easily hide under furniture in the direct line of sight of smaller infants and babies. One excellent safety measure is to only allow your older child to play with more intricate toys while the younger child is napping or in a separate room with a closed door. Utilize higher storage for these toys and make sure that they are put away immediately after use. The only toys you should leave at easy reach for your infant or toddler would be age-appropriate toys inspected for any easily removable parts.

Choking Hazards

The AAP has a good review on choking hazards[10], and it specifically lists some of the most dangerous objects. The list includes latex balloons, balls, marbles, and spherical toys or toy parts. Balloons are the leading cause of non-food choking death in children, and most occur in children younger than age six. Reportedly, a minimum of 68 children died from choking on latex balloons from 1990 through 2004 in the U.S. and they are responsible for 29% of overall choking deaths in children. Broken pieces are higher risk because they can form airtight seals on the airway and become difficult to dislodge with a cough or Heimlich maneuver. Playing with balloons should always be done under supervision at any age! It is best to not let young children try to inflate balloons and *never* allow them to bite balloons or put inflated balloons close to their mouths. This all being said, balloons are an object many children play with multiple times a year and provide a ton of fun when done safely. Aside from establishing rules about not inflating or biting, promptly clean up any broken pieces from a popped balloon, including water balloons. Mylar balloons are often a safer option because they are different than the more common latex balloons.

The AAP policy statement on the *Prevention of Choking Among Children* makes some important points about toy safety.[10] Risky objects include balls, marbles, and spherical toys because they are round or cylindrical and can slide in easily, especially if they are roughly the same diameter or size as a child's mouth or throat. The U.S. Consumer Product Safety Commission (CPSC) is responsible for choking-hazard warning labels on toys or other materials.[11] The CPSC requires labels on toys and objects that have "small parts," which are defined by the small-parts test fixture (SPTF). The SPTF simulates the mouth and throat dimensions of a child.[10] There are defined dimensions. For instance, balls must be at least 1.75 inches in diameter or larger to be sold for the use by children younger than three. The AAP policy statement reports that a review of 101 foreign bodies (i.e. random objects) that caused a choking death in children under the age of three showed that 14 of the toys had passed minimum safety requirements for use in those children. Likewise, they draw attention to the fact that the CPSC does not conduct premarket testing of toys, meaning that safety is not guaranteed for a toy just because it can be sold on the U.S market.[10]

Importantly, the most common reason for a toy to be recalled by the CPSC is a previously unrecognized choking hazard. However, typically only 10% to 30% of toys are returned after recalls, though this excludes the possibility that parents are just throwing the toy away rather than returning it. The most important takeaway is to review all the toys that come into your home to identify if there is a potential risk. Look for spherical shaped objects that could block a child's airway or loose pieces. Check second-hand or older toys for any damaged pieces that may become a hazard as well. As a new child is born or reaches a new mobility milestone, such as the ability to crawl or stand, review toys currently in the household to confirm they are still appropriately stored and available only to the appropriate ages. Your five-year-old might be okay to play with a certain toy, but your newly walking 14-month-old may not be.

As for food, hot dogs are the most common culprit because of their cylindrical shape that approximates the size of the airway, responsible for up to 17% of food related choking deaths.[10] Other risky foods according to a study in 1984 include[12]:

- Hard candy
- Peanuts/nuts
- Seeds
- Whole grapes
- Raw carrots
- Apples
- Popcorn
- Peanut butter chunks
- Marshmallows
- Chewing gum
- Sausages

Window Blinds and Cords

Window blinds and cords are a risk for strangulation as well. This is different than choking but is included under the same umbrella for the purposes of the CDC WISQARS statistics One review found approximately 16,800 window blind injuries occurred from 1990-2015.[13] Approximately 12% of these injuries were related to entanglement, 81% of which involved the neck, and 99% of entanglement injuries were caused by window blind cords. The U.S. CPSC estimates 8 children under the age of 5 die yearly from strangulation in window blinds.[14] This is not an insignificant risk. Children often reach for something to hold onto like the blinds or cords without realizing the potential danger that can quickly occur. The best way to prevent window cord strangulation is to replace all blinds in your dwelling with cordless blinds. While this may not be specifically cheap, it is the safest way to address this issue. I will admit that we have not replaced our blinds in our current house with cordless blinds, but we do make sure all blinds are wrapped carefully and placed high out of reach for our children. Safety wraps and cord holders are also readily available to keep cords out of reach of children so consider this feature when childproofing. They are available online at Amazon and other retailers.

Don't Forget About the Car

As discussed in chapter 5, be aware of choking risks in the car. Take caution when allowing your children to eat in the car, at least at younger ages. There is no formal guidance on what age is appropriate, but I would suggest waiting until the child can feed themselves appropriately in the highchair or dinner table with only safe foods, such as small crackers. Be careful when your child is still in a rear-facing car seat. A child in a rear-facing car seat may not alert you to their distress, and while mirrors can help with monitoring the backseat, focus should remain on driving. You cannot directly observe your children while you are driving, and it could be very difficult to reach your child quickly if a choking event were to happen. Not to mention, stopping on the side of the road can have its own dangers. Toys that are choking hazards should be avoided. Liquids are less concerning.

Summary

Choking and strangulation should be taken seriously. That does not mean you have to be high stress or high alert all the time. PREVENTION is the first goal. Read on what your child is allowed to eat at what age, and restrict access to choking hazards like toys from older children. Then you don't have to be as stressed about it. For the situation when your child inevitably does choke on something, make sure you don't panic because it doesn't help anyone. Go to a CPR class, and make sure you occasionally review the steps. Most choking episodes are not fatal, but make sure your child is breathing and playing normally shortly afterward, because persistent partial blockages can occur. Concerning window blinds, replace them with cordless blinds if possible but at least keep all cords out of reach of your small children. Don't let your younger toddlers and infants eat in the car. Keep these things in mind, and you can make your life easier and your child safer.

* * *

References

1. Sivakumar S, Prabhu A. Physiology, Gag Reflex. *StatPearls*. 2024.

2. Choking First Aid and Prevention in Children. Cleveland Clinic: Health Essentials. Updated June 26, 2023. Accessed August 27, 2027. https://health.clevelandclinic.org/choking-first-aid-prevention

3. Warning Letter to Dechoker LLC. U.S. Food & Drug Administration. Updated May 10, 2021. Accessed September 18, 2024. https://www.fda.gov/inspections-compliance-enforcement-and-criminal-investigations/warning-letters/Dechoker-llc-614629-05102021

4. Ramaswamy A, Done A, Solis R, Srikanth M, Olinde L, Belafsky P. The efficacy of two commercially available devices for airway foreign body relief: A cadaver study. *Laryngoscope Investig Otolaryngol*. Jun 2023;8(3):708-711. doi:10.1002/lio2.1057

5. Patterson E, Tang HT, Ji C, Perkins GD, Couper K. The efficacy and usability of suction-based airway clearance devices for foreign body airway obstruction: a manikin randomised crossover trial. *Resusc Plus*. Mar 2021;5:100067. doi:10.1016/j.resplu.2020.100067

6. Dunne CL, Osman S, Viguers K, Queiroga AC, Szpilman D, Peden AE. Phase One of a Global Evaluation of Suction-Based

Airway Clearance Devices in Foreign Body Airway Obstructions: A Retrospective Descriptive Analysis. *Int J Environ Res Public Health.* Mar 24 2022;19(7)doi:10.3390/ijerph19073846

7. Dunne CL, Viguers K, Osman S, Queiroga AC, Szpilman D, Peden AE. A 2-year prospective evaluation of airway clearance devices in foreign body airway obstructions. *Resusc Plus.* Dec 2023;16:100496. doi:10.1016/j.resplu.2023.100496

8. Choking Hazards. Center for Disease Control: Nutrition. Updated February 25, 2022. Accessed August 27, 2024. https://www.cdc.gov/nutrition/InfantandToddlerNutrition/foods-and-drinks/choking-hazards.html

9. Choking Prevention for Babies & Children. HealthyChildren.org. Updated August 23, 2024. Accessed August 27, 2024. https://www.healthychildren.org/English/health-issues/injuries-emergencies/Pages/Choking-Prevention.aspx

10. Committee on Injury V, Poison P. Prevention of choking among children. *Pediatrics.* Mar 2010;125(3):601-7. doi:10.1542/peds.2009-2862

11. Small Parts ban and Choking Hazard Labeling. U.S. Consumer Product Safety Commission. Accessed September 18, 2024. https://www.cpsc.gov/Business--Manufacturing/Business-Education/Business-Guidance/Small-Parts-for-Toys-and-Childrens-Products

12. Harris CS, Baker SP, Smith GA, Harris RM. Childhood asphyxiation by food. A national analysis and overview. *JAMA.* May 4 1984;251(17):2231-5.

13. Onders B, Kim EH, Chounthirath T, Hodges NL, Smith GA. Pediatric Injuries Related to Window Blinds, Shades, and Cords. *Pediatrics.* Jan 2018;141(1)doi:10.1542/peds.2017-2359

14. Window Covering Cords. U.S. Consumer Product Safety Commission. Accessed August 27, 2024. https://www.cpsc.gov/gocordless

Chapter 11

Poison and Ingestion

I swallowed a quarter when I was around two years of age. My mother spilled her coin purse, and I got to it before she could. She noticed I was having difficulty breathing and I was hoarse, her mom instincts and nurse training kicked in, and she put two and two together. Shortly afterward, a physician retrieved the quarter with a scope from where it was stuck in my esophagus. I'm sure there are many stories of similar incidents. Many ingested objects, including smaller coins like dimes and pennies, will pass through without incident. But when should you be concerned?

I've lumped poisoning and ingestion together to mean the child has swallowed something potentially harmful for sake of simplicity. In this section, I'm referring to *poisoning* as the swallowing of a medication or chemical that is harmful, whereas the term *ingestion* implies a foreign body, such as a toy or coin, has been swallowed. Poisoning is estimated at 886,000 to 1,000,000 events per year or more in ages 0-5 based on reporting to the American Association of Poison Control Centers.[1] The vast majority of poisonings, over 90%, occur in the home. Despite the high number of events reported, the number of deaths by unintentional poisoning are low. In 2019, the numbers reported were 17 deaths in children under age 1, 27 deaths in ages 1-4, 12 in ages 5-9, and 21 in ages 10-14. These numbers do include non-oral poisoning, such as carbon monoxide and pesticide exposures. Even though it did not crack our top five causes of non-medical deaths for two of these age groups, it still is an event to be aware of because non-fatal exposure is such a common occurrence. As far as ingested foreign bodies go, approximately 100,000 cases are reported in the U.S. each year and more than 75% occur in children.[2] Fortunately, fatality is rare with this event.

As with many of our topics, the primary key for the category of oral poisoning is prevention. Here's the checklist:

1. Place all chemicals and medicines in your highest cabinets
2. Lock the cabinets that contain toxic substances
3. Get rid of opioid pain medications
4. Pick up spilled medications immediately

Let me begin with the following disclaimer: If you have any inclination that your child has eaten, swallowed, breathed, touched, or licked something they shouldn't and you are concerned, do not hesitate to ask for help or get them checked by a medical provider. The poison control center and ER have seen it all, and they will not judge or berate you for being cautious. There's no need to feel silly about asking for assistance, so err on the side of being overly cautious.

Prevention

It seems fairly simple, but if you place the danger out of reach to children, you can decrease your anxiety over this possibility. Our common areas where cleaning products are often stored, like under bathroom and kitchen counters, can present an exciting challenge for curious child. Common practice is to leave these chemicals under sinks in bathrooms for convenient access, but children can get into these, even with lids that are thought to be secured. Medications, alcohol, nail polish remover, and hydrogen peroxide are all examples of solutions that are often kept in easily accessible areas in homes without young children. Child restraint locking mechanisms on medicine bottles are helpful, but older children may accept the challenge and get into medications they shouldn't. They may think they are getting one of their routine medications such as a vitamin but take the wrong pill instead. Teach your older children never to take medications on their own. Consider getting a lockable box or safe. Likewise, pick up any medications you accidentally spill immediately. Pills and capsules can often look like candy to small children. The same is true for garage chemicals as well. They should be kept up high and make sure the lids are secured appropriately.

One analysis of fatal poisonings in the US from 2005 to 2018 found 731 total fatalities in children ages 5 and under, 42% of which were in children less than 1 year old.[3] Approximately one-third of cases occurred while an individual other than a biological parent was supervising. Opioids were the cause of 47% of the deaths followed by over-the-counter pain, cold, and allergy medications at 14.8%. In 2005, opioids contributed to 24.1% of deaths whereas they contributed to 52.2% in 2018. This aligns with the opioid epidemic happening in the U.S. Many parents may have opioids still in the cabinet from a post-surgical prescription, particularly after a Cesarean section (C-section) for example. Once you are done with these, dispose of them. It's not worth the risk. (I could go on a rant here, but it's best to never take them to begin with, or at least two days maximum after surgery).

Keep the other medications locked in a cabinet up high. One study estimates approximately 9,500 children per year are hospitalized emergently for unsupervised medication ingestions, and often opioids and their derivatives are involved. This is a completely preventable event.[4] If you have adolescents, be aware of the potential for abuse. Have a discussion with your adolescents about drug abuse and the dangers of opioids and taking unknown pills. Unfortunately, recreational opioid use is on the rise, and teenagers may hear about the potential for euphoric "highs" that come from taking these medications. They may secretively seek them out in your household. Most have smaller bodies than adults and not be aware of the risk of death from overdose. They could accidentally overdose at any time, especially the first time taking such medications out of curiosity or because of peer pressure. Aside from locking your cabinets, you should dispose of medications appropriately (see section below).

Be particularly careful at the houses of other caregivers where your children spend a lot of time, such as the grandparents' houses. Unlocked pill boxes are commonly used in households for adults that take multiple medications daily, such as the weekly pill box sorters. One close friend of ours had to ask her father to stop putting medications in different bottles and adding his own labels because it was confusing and dangerous to himself and the children. Keep medications in their appropriate bottles, and get rid of them if the label fades or cannot be read. It's a good idea to check into the habits of your parents when you visit with regard to medications.

Prescription and Over-the-Counter Medications

Disposal of unused medications is recommended by the U.S. Food and Drug Administration (FDA). There is a list of medications that can be flushed safely down the toilet available on their website at: https://www.fda.gov/drugs/disposal-unused-medicines-what-you-should-know/drug-disposal-fdas-flush-list-certain-medicines#Flush List.[5] They also have instructions for how to dispose of non-flushable medications in the trash, which may involve mixing the medications with coffee grounds or dirt, for example. A list is available on their website at: https://www.fda.gov/drugs/disposal-unused-medicines-what-you-should-know/drug-disposal-dispose-non-flush-list-medicine-trash If you have any such medications, I recommend visiting the FDA website to learn more about disposing of them.

Also, make sure you don't accidentally poison your child by giving them a medication that is age-inappropriate or the inappropriate dose. Stick to labels on the bottles and do some research on medications that are safe for your child at certain ages if you feel a non-prescription medication is needed. When leaving your child in the care of another caregiver, make sure to provide a list of any medications they might need to dispense along with your child's weight and doses. One helpful tip is to provide a syringe with a line drawn by Sharpie to indicate the correct dose and provide different syringes for each child. Label the syringes as well. It might be a good idea to keep this at your own house as well to keep everything separate.

Carbon Monoxide

Carbon monoxide is a common source of fatality in children with poisoning, though this is due to inhalation rather than oral intake. Carbon monoxide is an odorless, colorless gas, so you won't smell it or see it.

Be aware of the common symptoms of carbon monoxide poisoning in either yourself or your child:

- headache
- dizziness
- weakness
- nausea
- vomiting
- chest pain
- confusion

I've mentioned earlier about motor vehicles being the primary source of this, so do not let your child sit in the car in the garage with it running. Do not let any motor vehicle (lawn mower, leaf blower, etc.) sit running in a garage even if the door is open. You should have at least one carbon monoxide detector in your house, preferably in areas of high risk, such as the kitchen or near a furnace. If it goes off, leave your house immediately and call a specialist. Many homes, particularly in the colder parts of the U.S., are heated with furnaces, which pose a higher risk. Around Christmas a few years ago in one of our homes, our furnace started putting out carbon monoxide, and the only way we knew about it was our carbon monoxide detector. Use carbon monoxide detectors in your place of dwelling.

Boats can be a source of carbon monoxide poisoning. If you are using or playing on a boat, you should make sure a monitor is installed if there is an enclosed cabin on board. Rear swim decks or swimming behind the boat when the engine is idling can be dangerous. Likewise, you should not let the boat sit idling for very long, and you should anchor or dock your boat at least 20 feet away from the nearest boat if it is running a generator or its engine.[7]

Poison Control

What should you do if an exposure happens or if you suspect your child ingested a chemical? Call a poison control center. There are 55 centers, one for each state and some of the territories in the U.S., like Puerto Rico. The number is 1-800-222-1222. In an emergency, you could look this number up more quickly online, but I've included it here for reference. Consider adding it to your cell phone contact list for quick and easy emergency access. The poison control center will direct you on how to proceed, such as monitoring the child or to take them to the nearest Emergency Department. Even ER physicians contact poison control centers because the centers keep a running list of all the ingested materials and their potential harm to children. They will also time and track poison exposure for you and give you updates. Sometimes physicians must administer chemicals to induce vomiting or help absorb some of the excess substance. Sometimes children need to be monitored with blood work for a few days.

Foreign Bodies

The most commonly ingested foreign body is a coin, responsible for 80% of cases that required removal of the object by a scope procedure.[8] Other common objects include button batteries, straight pins, needles, fish bones, earrings, magnets, and water beads. The good news is that death from *ingested* foreign body is rare. In fact, foreign bodies are more likely to cause death by *suffocation*, or blockage of the airway. Assuming the object has already gotten past the airway, the majority will pass on their own out into a diaper or toilet in the stool. Only 10-20% of objects require endoscopic removal (non-invasive procedure with a scope down the esophagus) and less than 1% require open surgical intervention.[2]

Most Emergency Room (ER) visits due to ingested foreign bodies occur because the event was witnessed by someone. Here are some signs of potential ingestion if you have not witnessed an event but are suspicious:

- Trouble swallowing food
- Drooling
- Pain in the neck or chest
- Coughing
- Trouble breathing
- Noisy breathing

However, most cases are without symptoms at all.

You should never have to worry about the decision to have the foreign body removed. Leave that to a physician. Go to the emergency room if you're suspicious a child swallowed something they shouldn't have. You could call your pediatrician during business hours, but they will likely refer you to an ER. You should call 911 if the child is having difficulty breathing or is drooling, but otherwise your own vehicle should be safe.

For education purposes, we will discuss below what typically is performed based on the scenario. You should *never* make this decision on your own and you should *never* use this book to try to avoid an ER visit for the following examples. *Always* take a child to an ER as quickly as possible if you suspect an event. Coins are most often found in the stomach by the time of the initial X-ray.[2] If coins are in the stomach, they are allowed to pass and are monitored. If they are stuck in the esophagus, they are usually allowed an attempt at passing spontaneously (i.e. own their own) as long as the child is not having difficulty breathing and they can swallow otherwise.

Batteries are never allowed to remain in the esophagus. They are a true emergency because they contain caustic materials, and they can essentially become activated by your saliva. This will cause a small electric current which can kill the surrounding tissue and potentially create a hole in the esophagus. This can occur as quickly as eight hours after the ingestion. Once they reach the stomach, however, they are typically allowed to be monitored for spontaneous passage and are usually harmless.

Sharp objects are typically removed due to higher risk of perforation, i.e. creating a hole in the esophagus. Magnets are high-risk objects, particularly if more than one is swallowed. Magnets can attract and connect from different spots within the small intestines and pinch the soft intestinal tissues between the two magnets. This can create a hole within hours of the magnetic connection. Even single magnets can pose a risk and are sometimes removed if easily accessible.

Water beads are a very popular toy. They start as small spheres slightly smaller than grains of rice but become significantly larger when placed in water. With the increase in popularity, there has also been an increase in ingestion events and danger to children. Be *extremely* careful with these around children. They look like candy and are very small. They can be tempting to toddlers. If ingested, they can expand and block certain tighter passages in the intestinal tract. If a known ingestion has occurred, removal is usually recommended.

Button Batteries

When you come home from a birthday party with a bag of fun, small toys, how many of them light up or make noises? These light wands, flashing balls, and necklaces often contain button batteries, which pose a huge risk if ingested because of their size and likelihood of becoming trapped in the esophagus. You should monitor and inspect any new toys that come into your home and educate caregivers on these risks as well. Household items like remotes and scales can also have these small batteries. Keep replacement batteries in a secure location. Make sure that toys with battery compartments have the screws securely in place. If the screw is lost, throw the toy away or do not use any batteries with it.

Summary

In summary, prevention is your best bet. Secure your coins and batteries up high away from children. Keep medications up high and in a locked area. Dispose of medications that you no longer are taking, particularly opioids. Keep all lids secured. If you suspect a chemical has been ingested, call poison control. If you suspect an object has been ingested, go to the ER promptly to get an evaluation. Do not try to make medical decisions on your own. The best way to avoid this risk is appropriate storage. My wife and I take appropriate precautions to keep these things out of our children's reach, and it keeps me from worrying about it.

* * *

References

1. Kelly N. Prevention of poisoning in children. UpToDate. Updated July 9, 2024. Accessed August 27, 2024. https://www.uptodate.com/contents/prevention-of-poisoning-in-children#!

2. Gilger M. Foreign bodies of the esophagus and gastrointestinal tract in children. UpToDate. Updated July 29, 2024. Accessed August 27, 2024.

3. Gaw CE, Curry AE, Osterhoudt KC, Wood JN, Corwin DJ. Characteristics of Fatal Poisonings Among Infants and Young Children in the United States. *Pediatrics*. Apr 1 2023;151(4)doi:10.1542/peds.2022-059016

4. Lovegrove MC, Mathew J, Hampp C, Governale L, Wysowski DK, Budnitz DS. Emergency hospitalizations for unsupervised prescription medication ingestions by young children. *Pediatrics*. Oct 2014;134(4):e1009-16. doi:10.1542/peds.2014-0840

5. Drug Disposal: FDA's Flush List for Certain Medicines. U.S. Food & Drug Administration. Updated October 1, 2020. Accessed August 27, 2024. https://www.fda.gov/drugs/disposal-unused-medicines-what-you-should-know/drug-disposal-fdas-flush-list-certain-medicines#FlushList

6. Drug Disposal: Dispose "Non-Flush List" Medicine in Trash. U.S. Food & Drug Administration. Updated December 20, 2018. Accessed August 27, 2024. https://www.fda.gov/drugs/disposal-unused-medicines-what-you-should-know/drug-disposal-dispose-non-flush-list-medicine-trash

7. About CO Poisoning on Your Boat. Center for Disease Control: Carbon Monoxide Poisoning. Updated April 10, 2024. Accessed August 27, 2024. https://www.cdc.gov/carbon-monoxide/about/boating.html

8. Denney W, Ahmad N, Dillard B, Nowicki MJ. Children will eat the strangest things: a 10-year retrospective analysis of foreign body and caustic ingestions from a single academic center. *Pediatr Emerg Care*. Aug 2012;28(8):731-4. doi:10.1097/PEC.0b013e31826248eb

Chapter 12

Firearms

Firearms are a hot button topic with politicians, especially during election season, but the fact remains that firearms are a common part of life for many people in the U.S. The number of firearms in the U.S. is currently estimated at approximately 393 million owned by citizens.[1] In context, firearm deaths are common as an overall cause of death but certainly from a *relative* standpoint, they really are not as common as you might expect given the number of firearms. Guns do *not* kill people. People kill people using guns as a weapon, whether intentional or accidental. Children are no different. Just like you wouldn't want a child to get your car keys and drive off with your car, you don't want them to have any sort of access to a firearm.

With respect to children, at least one third of children live in a home with firearms. Forty-three percent of these homes contain at least 1 firearm that is loaded and unlocked.[2] This section is focused on the prevention of firearm related deaths in children. Deaths include accidental discharge as well as suicide, with most of the deaths in ages over 10 being from suicide. The AAP Advocacy statement on pediatric firearm injuries states that the most reliable way to prevent death from firearms in children is to have complete absence of guns in the household.[3] Though it is perhaps theoretically the most reliable way, many people do own firearms and maintain them safely within their homes. Even if you do *not* own a firearm or do not plan on owning one, this chapter is worth a read because gun safety should be promoted regardless, and your child may visit a home with firearms present.

When discussing firearm injuries and death in this chapter, recall that my focus is mostly on ages 0 through 10, but I will discuss adolescent and teenagers at times, and the prevention strategies are still valid for all ages under the age of 18, when you can legally purchase a firearm. Some resources will point to gun deaths as being the biggest threat to children but make sure you are aware of what age groups they are including, because often those statistics will include age groups up through age 20 or 24. For instance, the AAP Technical Report on firearm injuries in children and youth cites 10,197 deaths in the year 2020 for ages 0-24, which is greater than the number of motor vehicle-related deaths for that year at 8,309.[4] This age group includes young adults, including many over the age of 18. Many firearm-related deaths are from intentional suicide, and the older age groups are their own animal because of intentional gun violence as independently living adults. Intentional gun violence in the older age groups is outside the scope of my book, so I will focus on the younger ages.

Accidental vs. Intentional on the Statistic Sheet

Intentional gun violence shows up on WISQARS statistics as a homicide or suicide. As discussed in a subsequent chapter, *homicide* usually does not include accidental discharge as far as I can tell on the CDC's tallies. It's difficult to separate out the homicide tallies in terms of whether the firearm was used to intentionally kill someone or if it was accidental because the CDC statistics are based on something called the International Classification of Diseases (ICD). If you know any physicians, you'll know ICD coding is the bane of our existence. You'll often hear us complain about this system. It is essentially how we code all medical problems with our documentation. We are currently on the tenth iteration of this system, and they've exploded the number of codes. The system is really supposed to be helpful for epidemiology studies and statistics, but because the (I'm sure entirely respectable) overlords have expanded the codes so much, it has gotten difficult to accurately code certain medical events.

As an example of the coding system, if someone breaks their humerus (arm bone), there are 9 different ways to initially code just a fracture of the top part of the humerus (i.e. the shoulder). Then you must specify left and right, which doubles the number of codes. Then you must add whether this fracture is displaced or nondisplaced (so that's now up to 36 codes for this injury). Then you must state whether this is the initial visit, subsequent visit (further subdivided into essentially appropriate healing, delayed healing, not healing), or sequela of (meaning complication of or as a result of the injury). So now we're up to over 100 codes for just fractures in the top part of the humerus. Seriously. This does not include the shaft of the bone or the elbow part of the humerus because the bone is divided into three segments. That means there are at least triple the number of codes for the humerus alone, just one bone. (Can you understand our frustration with this system???)

For the most part, the specific code is completely irrelevant to how I actually treat a patient, so there are times when codes get slightly improperly documented just because of the imperfection of search engines we use to code during our documentation. For that reason, I think the system is completely flawed because it's too complicated. Regardless, that's how we track data. (Don't hate the player, hate the game!)

The ICD codes with firearms seem to revolve around "assault by firearm" and "discharge by firearm." With the CDC WISQARS homicide tallies, firearm deaths are labeled as "assault by firearm," which is likely coded by an ER physician, medical examiner, or coroner to document the event. There is potential for crossover between categories based on the coder being unfamiliar with the system and an "Assault" code is picked even if it's an accident and vice versa. The code that gets defaulted into the *Unintentional Injury* category on WISQARS is labeled as "discharge by firearm" whereas "assault by firearm" gets recorded as a *Homicide*. These codes and descriptions are so vague that there is certainly some crossover. Regardless, it doesn't change the fact that accidental deaths by firearm happen in children. It just means that death statistics labeled as accidental or intentional may be mixed up somewhat.

Let's address the accidental deaths; we will discuss suicide and intentional homicide deaths in subsequent chapters. There were 24 children ages 1-4 killed by accidental firearm discharge in 2019, fewer than 12 deaths in ages 5-9, 16 deaths in ages 10-14, and 128 deaths in ages 15-24. Thankfully, despite the number of children living in homes with loaded and unlocked firearms, the death rate from accidental discharge is relatively low when you think about it. For deaths by firearm-related homicide (theoretically intentional though not explicitly stated), the tallies are 47 for ages 1-4, 68 for ages 5-9, 144 for ages 10-14, and 4,339 deaths in ages 15-24. Again, the CDC splits these apart but it's difficult to know for sure based on the coding, so I include both the recorded accidental and intentional shooting deaths.

Defining the Problem

To further describe the issue, I'm going to quote some statistics adopted from *Everytown*, a research group dedicated to gun safety. From 2015 through 2022 there were 2,802 accidental shootings by children 17 and younger.[5] Most of these are in the age group from 14-17, which should make sense because these are the ages where access becomes easier and more tempting for sport as well as the age when intentional violence becomes a problem. Note that not all these result in death. Some range from minor wounds all the way to severely disabling wounds (nerve or spinal cord injury, for example).

Likewise, it is important to consider who is actually *shooting* the victim. *Everytown* cites there were 895 preschoolers and toddlers aged 5 and under during this 7-year span who managed to shoot themselves or someone else unintentionally. Children at that age would be extremely unlikely to be purposefully shooting with intent to harm, meaning these are nearly all accidental. Nine hundred thirty-three children under 5 were shot during this same 7-year time period. The above data indicates that the majority of these incidences are not coming from adults accidentally shooting children, but rather *children shooting each other*. This is completely preventable with appropriate precautions. Alarmingly, during this time span, while shootings from ages 14-17 *decreased* by 28%, shootings in the 5 and under age range *increased* over time by 33%.

In most of the data in this book, I've been reviewing the year 2019 specifically because it was pre-COVID. It is worth mentioning that *Everytown* notes that 2020 and 2021 had increasing rates of shooting post-COVID. This is probably due to more children being at home during that time with potentially more access. Many parents were also more likely to be doing shooting sports on their time off during lockdowns, which probably contributed to more access from guns being out of their safes more often. By the way, 81% of shooters were boys and 76% of victims were boys and men, so you have to be especially careful if you have sons.[6] Seventy percent of unintentional shootings by children occur in a home. Do you see the problem? This is an easily preventable cause of death in children if you take a few easy steps as a gun owner. Likewise, you must be careful about the houses of others that your child might visit.

Considering the last paragraph, my main focus for this book is accidental deaths by children and how we can prevent them as parents. Teenage intentional violence is its own animal. Certainly, mass shootings are a major health topic right now, but that's outside the scope of this book. Mass shootings are a very well publicized issue in this nation, particularly school shootings. Despite the publicity for these events, your child is statistically more likely to die from an accidental gunshot by a friend or by their own hand, and this fact is probably not as well publicized because it happens sporadically and randomly. I say this to call attention to and redirect you to something you can control within your own child's life and personal sphere of influence.

Your child is still more likely to die or be injured by a motor vehicle crash, but some of that risk is unavoidable. You can only do your best to drive safely and secure your child appropriately. With accidental gun trauma, you absolutely have more control over this. All it takes is awareness. If we as a nation pay so much attention to mass shootings when they come around and argue about how to prevent them, then we should pay equal lip service to advertising how to prevent isolated accidental shootings by children, which cause more loss of life on average than school shootings. Logically it follows that most injuries with young children are caused by handguns rather than rifles or shotguns, at least with self-harm. Rifles and shotguns are harder to lift and aim for children, but rifles and shotguns can still be dangerous.

Securing Firearms

The biggest advice I can give is to *secure your firearms*. This is accomplished by three major ways:

1. Locked safes for firearms
2. Locked ammo in separate containers
3. Trigger locks

The more of these steps you add, the harder it is to use a firearm. It's that simple. No access means no problem. These steps have been shown to be more effective than education programs.[7] Even children that have been taught how to address weapons in the home with multiple education programs are capable and even likely to pick up weapons they see lying around. The safest option is to keep them from ever being able to fire the gun. In other words, assume that your child will touch the gun regardless of their knowledge of safety around guns. Assume they will touch the gun if they see it even if they know not to. In fact, this has been shown in several studies.[8-10] Find a way to make it so they physically cannot fire the gun. That's your best and safest bet if you own a firearm.

Many people want the security of a firearm in their house that they can quickly access in case of an emergency. The tendency is to leave a loaded weapon somewhere easily accessible for an adult and hidden. Just remember, children can reach high places easier than you think. They make safes that have quick fingerprint or code access. This is probably the best way to combine easy access for emergencies yet reduce the risk of your child accessing the weapon. This is an expensive option, but I think it is worth it for the safety of your family. Additionally, even if you keep one in a safe, it's best to keep it unloaded because that's at least one more error away from your child accidentally discharging the weapon. The best practice is to have a separate ammo container that is also locked. You are twice removing the access with two separately locked necessities to accidental discharge: the firearm itself and the ammo required. Finally, trigger locks provide an additional blockade to accidental discharge. These are possibly the cheapest option. They require a code or a key similar to a luggage lock before being released and allowing access to the trigger. Certainly, each one of these three options is exponentially helpful in isolation, but why not all three in combination?

More safety devices are available for handguns as well. This includes grip safety devices that require compression of a lever prior to firing the weapon, making it more difficult for a child to fire the weapon because they are too weak to squeeze it while simultaneously pulling the trigger. There are firing pin blocks that prevent the weapon from discharging if the gun is accidentally dropped on its hammer. They even make weapons that have fingerprint recognition and other devices that allow only the owner to fire the weapon.[7] Some weapons have magazine disconnect devices that keep the weapon from discharging if the magazine is not present.

If purchasing a firearm for self-defense, my advice would be to avoid a double-action revolver. Double-action revolvers typically require a single hard pull on the trigger, whereas semi-automatic pistols require the slide to be pulled back to load the weapon, which is very difficult for a child to do, and single action revolvers require the hammer to be cocked first. Double-action revolvers do not require an extra step. Handguns are the cause of 86% of unintentional shootings, so take this seriously.[5]

The Homes of Friends and Family

You can control risk in your own house but check with family members as well. One of our family members used to keep a loaded revolver in the top drawer of their dresser with their socks. I had to have a serious conversation with the family member because our children spent a lot of time at this house and also spent a lot of unattended time specifically in that bedroom when playing. All it would take is a nearby stool (and there was one in the bathroom) and a curious child (as they all are) to potentially find this weapon within reach. Likewise, the gun was a loaded double-action revolver, which only requires a hard pull on the trigger to fire. This was about as unsafe as you could make this firearm for child safety. Family members without young children in the house do not typically worry as much about these details but check with family members to ensure their households are safe as well. Additionally, beware of loaded firearms that are accessible in vehicles.

In fact, most accidental and intentional self-inflicted firearm injuries in children are caused using firearms from the child's home or the home of a friend or relative.[11,12] More than one third of unintentional shootings occur in the home of a friend, relative, or neighbor according to healthychildren.org.[13] *Healthy Children* recommends you ask questions about unlocked and/or loaded firearms being present in the home of a new playmate or relative that you are visiting for the first time, in the same way you might ask about pets, allergies, and adult supervision on your "first playdate" checklist.

Discuss with Your Children

Education is important, regardless of whether you own firearms. I'm sure everyone reading this book can recall fire safety tips from their elementary school teacher: "stop, drop, and roll." In a similar way, it's a good idea to teach your child to always tell an adult if they see a firearm and to *never* touch it. This works for younger children, but adolescents and teenagers may need to be educated more than that. Depending on your circumstances, it might be a good idea to send your child to a local education class on handling firearms if you plan on allowing them to use firearms for hunting or sport, for instance. Responsible behavior around firearms should be reinforced by parents. It doesn't matter if you don't own a firearm; the chances are high that your child will be able to access one as a teenager if desired.

Many children have exposure to guns through media, including video games. Likewise, toy guns are prevalent, and a real gun might seem like a toy to a child, especially as toys have become more realistic. They might not recognize the harm that guns can cause in real life or have an unfounded confidence in handling guns. As stated above, they should be taught to leave it alone and tell an adult immediately. Communication with your child is the best prevention tool for when they are outside of your home.

It is extremely important to note, however, that education alone is not enough. A study from 2002 had 34 children ages 4 to 7 participate in a week-long firearm safety program and compared them to 36 children who did not undergo the program.[9] The children were placed in pairs in a protected area with an unloaded semiautomatic pistol. Fifty-three percent of the pairs played with the gun, and the group that had undergone the week-long safety program did not fare any better than the other group.

Another study observed 29 groups of boys aged 8 to 12.[10] They were paired with 1 to 2 other boys (sibling or playmate) and observed in a room with a one-way mirror for 15 minutes for a total of 64 boys. The room had two water pistols and an unloaded handgun concealed in separate drawers. The handgun even had a radio transmitter that activated when the trigger was depressed with sufficient force to fire the gun. Twenty-one of the 29 groups discovered the pistol, of which approximately half of them did not know whether the gun was real or a toy. Sixteen of the groups touched the pistol. Sixteen of the boys pulled the trigger hard enough to discharge the firearm. Surprisingly, 90% of the boys who handled the firearm reported having background education in gun safety. Therefore, while education is important, removing access is the best prevention measure.

Self Defense

What about the event when an intruder breaks into your home and you need protection? I understand the argument about having a firearm nearby for self-defense. I cannot find great statistics on how often firearms are used in home self-defense so I cannot compare the relative consequences to those of accidental discharge by children. I believe you can both keep a firearm quickly available for self-defense *and* keep it safe from children if you take the steps I've mentioned above. It might add a few more seconds to your "response time" in an emergency, but I personally believe it would be worth it, particularly if you're keeping a single firearm specifically designated for this purpose. Sleeping with a gun is an absolute no-no. I also recommend other safety features such as an installed alarm system that notifies emergency personnel or a camera system like *Ring* or *Blink* to monitor your home for threats.

Summary

Firearms do not have to be a significant risk to your child. If you want to reduce stress in your household, limiting access makes it so that you don't have to worry about it as long as you follow some simple rules and make sure to always follow the rules when you are placing firearms back into their safes. Likewise, if you make it a rule to always lock safes after use and replace trigger locks, you don't have to worry about this issue with your child, at least in your dwelling. The Lord knows you have enough to worry about when caring for your child, so why not make this one easy and stress free? Just do it. Pick good habits and you won't regret it. Similarly, it is important to have a conversation with your child specifically about finding a gun in someone else's house. Teach them to leave it alone and immediately tell an adult.

* * *

References

1. McBride C. How Many Gun Owners are in America? (2024 Statistics). Ammo.com. Updated 2024. Accessed August 27, 2024. https://ammo.com/articles/how-many-gun-owners-in-america

2. Safe Storage of Firearms. American Academy of Pediatrics Advocacy. Updated January 26, 2024. Accessed August 27, 2024. https://www.aap.org/en/advocacy/state-advocacy/safe-storage-of-firearms/

3. Lee LK, Fleegler EW, Goyal MK, et al. Firearm-Related Injuries and Deaths in Children and Youth: Injury Prevention and Harm Reduction. *Pediatrics*. Oct 8 2022;doi:10.1542/peds.2022-060070

4. Lee LK, Fleegler EW, Goyal MK, et al. Firearm-Related Injuries and Deaths in Children and Youth. *Pediatrics*. Oct 8 2022;doi:10.1542/peds.2022-060071

5. Preventable Tragedies: Unintentional Shootings by Children. Everytown Research & Policy. Updated April 26, 2023. Accessed August 27, 2024. https://everytownresearch.org/report/notanaccident/

6. Barrett JT, Lee LK, Monuteaux MC, Farrell CA, Hoffmann JA, Fleegler EW. Association of County-Level Poverty and Inequities With Firearm-Related Mortality in US Youth. *JAMA Pediatr.* Feb 1 2022;176(2):e214822. doi:10.1001/jamapediatrics.2021.4822

7. Naik-Mathuria B, Gill A. Firearm injuries in children: Prevention. UpToDate. Updated July 2024. Accessed August 27, 2024. https://www.uptodate.com/contents/firearm-injuries-in-children-prevention?search=gun%20children&source=search_result&selectedTitle=1~67&usage_type=default&display_rank=1

8. Baxley F, Miller M. Parental misperceptions about children and firearms. *Arch Pediatr Adolesc Med.* May 2006;160(5):542-7. doi:10.1001/archpedi.160.5.542

9. Hardy MS. Teaching firearm safety to children: failure of a program. *J Dev Behav Pediatr.* Apr 2002;23(2):71-6. doi:10.1097/00004703-200204000-00002

10. Jackman GA, Farah MM, Kellermann AL, Simon HK. Seeing is believing: what do boys do when they find a real gun? *Pediatrics.* Jun 2001;107(6):1247-50. doi:10.1542/peds.107.6.1247

11. Grossman DC, Reay DT, Baker SA. Self-inflicted and unintentional firearm injuries among children and adolescents: the source of the firearm. *Arch Pediatr Adolesc Med.* Aug 1999;153(8):875-8. doi:10.1001/archpedi.153.8.875

12. Hemenway D, Solnick SJ. Children and unintentional firearm death. *Inj Epidemiol.* 2015;2(1):26. doi:10.1186/s40621-015-0057-0

13. Schaechter J. Guns in the Home: How to Keep Kids Safe. HealthyChildren.org. Updated June 24, 2024. Accessed August 27, 2024. https://www.healthychildren.org/English/safety-prevention/at-home/Pages/Handguns-in-the-Home.aspx

Chapter 13

Fire Danger

Fires and burns are worth discussing. They rank number 5 on the non-medical causes of death in ages 1-4 at 75 deaths in 2019 and number 4 in ages 5-9 with 60 deaths. Burns can cause death by direct heat, inhalation, or in a delayed fashion from medical complications from loss of normal skin tissue or damage to the lungs. When certain percentages of the body are burned severely, the body cannot stay hydrated and becomes extremely susceptible to infection. There are specific designated burn centers throughout the United States where severe cases are taken. Burns can be a result of something like a house fire but can also be the result of burns from chemical spills, car crashes resulting in fires, or even wildfires or campfires.

Here is the prevention checklist for fires/burns:

1. Install smoke detectors (preferably ones that automatically dial EMS/911) and check batteries regularly
2. Review fire safety and exit plans with children

3. Fire ladders for 2nd story bedrooms
4. Obey standard precautions when having outdoor fires

Smoke Detectors

With respect to housefires, just like most of our safety topics, the key is precaution and planning if you want to reduce stress and reduce your risk. The National Fire Protection Association (NFPA) recommends installing smoke detectors in the following locations of your home:

- Inside each bedroom,
- Outside each sleeping area
- On every level of the home, including the basement.

The best practice is to have smoke detectors that are connected to a security system that automatically alerts Emergency Medical Services (EMS/911) when triggered. They can also be interconnected so that when one sounds, they all sound.[1] Fires can get out of hand quickly, so the earlier EMS is notified, the better. It carries a higher price tag for this feature, but it's certainly worth it, and it usually lowers the cost of your house insurance. If you are renting, make sure the landlord has appropriate smoke detectors/fire alarms installed.

Planning and Other Aides

Other safety tips include fire planning and fire ladders. Appropriate fire safety tips can be found at the American Red Cross website: https://www.redcross.org/get-help/how-to-prepare-for-emergencies/types-of-emergencies/fire.html.[2] A checklist is provided on their website as well.

Discuss a plan with your child. The American Red Cross fire

safety campaign recommends teaching your children two ways to exit the house to safety and to practice these routes. Smoke and heat typically rise, so it's best to stay as low as you can while exiting. I've never personally experienced it, but those who have will tell you even familiar house environments become difficult to navigate when smoke is everywhere. Another recommendation is to "get out and stay out," meaning never go back inside for people, pets, or objects once you are outside safely. You should also discuss a meeting place for everyone to go once they are outside the house. They also recommend showing your kids the sound the fire alarm makes so they learn to recognize it and get to safety.

The American Red Cross recommends you practice a two-minute drill to get everyone out because some house fires can burn that quickly. When selecting bedrooms for your children, if a windowed room is an option, give them that room. If you have bedrooms on the second story, equip each room with a fire ladder. These are easily stored chain ladders that can hang from a window. They can be stored in a box in the closet or under a child's bed. They don't take up much room and can easily be deployed so the child can climb down to safety. I also recommend teaching your child how to open a window or even break a window in an emergency at the appropriate age. A broken leg is also better than getting stuck in a fire. Most falls from the second story will not kill children (see Chapter 8), so in an absolute emergency, jumping is safer than staying if no ladder is available. Teach your children to aim for bushes or other soft landing spots if worse comes to worse. The American Red Cross also states that only 26% of families have practiced fire escape plans, so I highly recommend you practice with your children.[3]

Caution with Outdoor Fires

I don't want to sound too much like Smokey the Bear here, but take proper precautions if you are going to have a fire. This is more generic advice, but just make sure you're not having a fire in a windy atmosphere, especially if it's dry around. Always have a way to stop the fire (fire extinguisher or a water hose, for example) and *make sure all cinders are completely out before leaving a site*. Many a fire is started by leaving a site when the flames aren't actively burning and assuming the cinders are done burning. They can easily reignite. Make sure you cover them with sand, dirt, or water or close a lid over your firepit to completely extinguish fires. You don't want to catch your house on fire.

One of my best friends accidentally caught his roommate's HVAC unit on fire when trying to burn something small in his yard. After he burned his trash and put it out, he walked away. Unfortunately, the cinders were still hot and reignited after he left. The lawn care crew happened to be mowing his yard that day and noticed the fire and rang his doorbell. Luckily it only cost him an HVAC unit instead of the whole house because it was seen early. We laugh about it now, but he could have burnt his house down, and he was very fortunate.

As for children, educate them on the advice above, but specifically teach them the danger of cinders and to recognize that the fire pit will still be very hot after the actual flames die down. They should be made aware not to put things in the fire or to play with flammable liquids, such as gasoline or aerosol sprays.

Appliances and Fire Starters

It's best to periodically review your appliances as well. One of the biggest hazards is stovetops. The knobs can be "fun" for children to play with, so be sure to get covers and locks for the knobs. When cooking, face pan handles inward so that small children cannot reach up and grab them. Preferentially use rear stove tops when cooking. There are also fire blankets that you can purchase that can be used to cover and put out grease fires.

Once, my middle son turned on the stove for "fun" while leaving the house with his mother. He was 4 at the time, and I happened to be sitting on the couch. I smelled and saw smoke coming from the kitchen and ran in just as the fire alarm went off and automatically triggered an EMS call. We had a pizza stone on top of the stove, and it had caught on fire from the stove being on for a few minutes. We didn't know he had turned the stove on, and we were extremely fortunate I was at the house to put out the fire before it burned the house down.

Be aware of microwave ventilation and dryer ventilation. Have the dryer vents cleaned and inspected regularly. Some apartment and condominium units require regular inspections. Periodically update these appliances as able, or at least check for safety hazards with these appliances. The American Red Cross references that child-playing fires are the cause of most fire-related deaths in preschool-aged children.[3] That means that children typically are the source of the fire, so you should reduce access to items that could pose a risk, including matches, lighters, and candles. Matches and lighters should be stored in high areas that are hard to reach and possibly even in locked cabinets. When lighters are purchased, it's best to select ones that have robust child safety mechanisms. I let my oldest son try to use our lighter one day as an experiment, and at age 7 he did not have the strength to push the safety switch and pull the trigger simultaneously. If you want to burn candles, leave them high and out of reach and don't forget to put them out.

* * *

References

1. Installing and Maintaining Smoke Alarms. National Fire Protection Association (NFPA). Accessed August 27, 2024. https://www.nfpa.org/education-and-research/home-fire-safety/smoke-alarms/installing-and-maintaining-smoke-alarms

2. Home Fire Safety. American Red Cross. Accessed August 27,

2024. https://www.redcross.org/get-help/how-to-prepare-for-emergencies/types-of-emergencies/fire.html

3.Children and Home Fires. American Red Cross. Accessed August 27, 2024. https://www.redcross.org/content/dam/redcross/atg/PDF_s/Preparedness___Disaster_Recovery/Disaster_Preparedness/Home_Fire/FireChildrenFactSheet.pdf

Chapter 14

Homicide/Child Abuse

Homicide is defined as "a killing of one human being by another" by Merrian Webster. It does not always imply intent. In the case of death statistics, the CDC tends to use *homicide* as a term that implies some sort of intent. It is not completely clear on their website, but if a child were to be accidentally shot by their sibling, it appears to count as a death in the *Unintentional Injury* column rather than the *Homicide* column. Regardless, for our purposes we are going to discuss it as an *intentional* injury. Homicide is the second leading cause of death in children ages 1-9. For ages 1-4, it is responsible for more deaths than cancer.

Child abuse is a broad term because it includes physical harm, emotional abuse, neglect, and other forms of abuse. In fact, neglect is the most common form of abuse. If you are reading this book, I will assume that you are a caring and loving parent. You went out of the way to purchase and spend time reading this book for tips on how to prevent injury for your child, so I doubt your heart is in the wrong place. Education is one of the keys to prevent child abuse from killing a child. Despite loving your child, it can be easy to have a momentary lapse in judgment and get angry with your child. So, for this segment, we will first discuss the risks for child abuse occurrences and then follow with some warnings for situations for parents of younger children to avoid. Likewise, we will briefly discuss how medical providers are taught to recognize child abuse situations with the hope you will also be able to recognize if concerned.

Maybe you're reading this book and do not have a child yet but are expecting. Parenting is hard, especially if you have a difficult infant. You may not actually want to hurt your child, but you can do it accidentally in a momentary brain lapse. Do not let this happen. Many parents have felt this way before, so you are not alone. *Colic* is defined as excessive crying and is typically defined as more than three hours per day on more than three days per week.[1] Even if your child doesn't meet this definition, multiple episodes of crying in a day when you are already experiencing poor sleep may feel overwhelming.

If your infant is crying for what you feel like is an excessive amount of time, the first thing you should do is check for manageable causes of crying, such as hunger, pain, fatigue, or food sensitivities. Try feeding your infant to see if this resolves the crying. Check the baby to see if a piece of clothing or the diaper is too tight. Make sure there is not a piece of hair wrapped around a finger, toe, or the penis, which is called a hair tourniquet. Try to put the baby to sleep. Check the baby for a fever (temperature greater than 100.4°F) or other sign of illness. As a long-term solution, call your healthcare provider if you feel these episodes are becoming unmanageable. Sometimes food sensitivities cause infants to cry excessively due to irritation from foods/ingredients you ingest in your diet if breastfeeding or in the formula that you are feeding your baby.

If you have ruled the above things out and you still cannot console the infant and feel overwhelmed, the best advice I have is:

1. Put the baby or child somewhere safe

2. Walk away and take deep breaths
3. Get help if you need a longer break

This advice is supported by various parent resources.[1-3] For infants, they will not die if you simply lie them flat in their crib and walk away for 10 minutes. They will be just fine. For that matter, even 30 minutes or an hour won't kill them if that's what you need at an extreme moment (though do not do this routinely). A crying baby is not a sign that you're a bad parent. Sure, there are all sorts of recommendations for appropriate soothing depending on the age of the child, but if you are pushed to the brink, it's best to walk away. For toddlers, find a safe location to place them (room with no choking or climbing hazards, for example), and leave them alone and take a break. It's *okay* to do this (though not frequently). If you need help, get help. Use your spouse/partner, parents, siblings, friends, neighbors, or whoever you can get a hold of. If you're dealing with depression or thoughts of hurting your child, GET HELP. You should never feel ashamed of doing what's right for your child; it doesn't make you a bad person. Professional counselors are available by phone 24/7 at 1-800-4-A-CHILD (422-4453) if you need counseling.

Shaken Baby Syndrome

It is worth mentioning Shaken Baby Syndrome. This is a condition that happens when someone vigorously shakes an infant or young toddler. Brain damage can happen quickly, with only a few vigorous shakes. That's why you're better off putting your child down and walking away if you know you are at a breaking point. Young children's heads are relatively larger than their bodies compared to adults. They also lack the neck muscles to support the weights of their heads. They have softer tissues as well. Shaking a child back and forth creates a whiplash effect where the brain shifts inside of the skull quickly. This can damage the brain cells directly. The shaking event can also shear blood vessels that surround the brain, and they can bleed slowly, creating what's called a *subdural hematoma*, which is a pocket of blood. The hematoma expands and pushes on the brain, which causes further damage to the cells. Shaken Baby Syndrome can cause long term effects and even death in children. Head injury is the leading cause of death from child abuse under the age of 2, followed by abdominal trauma.[4] It goes without saying, commit to never shaking your baby or child out of anger.

Risk Factors

Risk factors for victims include children aged less than 4 and children with special needs.[5] Younger children can be more difficult to take care of (depending on the age of your children, I'm sure you know this). Some children do not sleep as well for the first year of life. Caring for children with special needs may carry unique emotional, psychological, and financial challenges. My wife and I do not have any children with special needs, so I cannot say this from personal experience. All I can say is that parenting a child *without* special needs is extremely difficult and taxing at times, and I can only imagine a special need adding a significant amount of difficulty. The best advice I have is to get as much social support as you can.[6]

Risk factors for perpetrators of child abuse include[5]:

- Caregivers with drug or alcohol issues
- Depression
- History of being abused
- Single parents
- Younger parents
- Lower education level or income level
- Non-biologically related caregivers[5]

A lot of these make sense, but it's difficult to resolve many of these complex issues with simple solutions, such as depression or alcohol dependence. You can't snap your fingers and make this go away. If this describes you, know yourself and your limits for when you need to ask for help. Though one source states biological parents are the most common perpetrators, be careful if you are leaving your child with a non-biological parent.[7] Does your partner have a history of drug or alcohol issues? It's best not to leave them alone with your child if you can avoid it. Do you need more help? Move closer to family or friends you know can help support you. While rare, physical child abuse can occur at daycares in certain circumstances. You may not necessarily be a danger to your child, but others can be, so try your best to avoid situations where there could be higher risk.

Other risk factors include a non-related adult living in the household, with one study showing that 83.9% of abuse cases were perpetrated by the non-related adult.[8] Also, death was 50 times more likely in such household living situations compared to children living with both biological parents and single parents. Likewise, episodes of child abuse are more likely in families with multiple unplanned births compared with no unplanned births, with one study estimating 2.8 times more likely.[9] Be aware if this describes your situation, and recognize that your child might be at higher risk.

Signs of Physical Abuse

Let's discuss a few quick medical tidbits on child abuse for recognition. Skin lesions are the most common signs of child abuse, including bruises, scratches, and burns. When reviewing injuries for potential cases of child abuse, certain fracture patterns are only possible with child abuse because of twisting mechanisms that simply don't happen because of a simple fall. Other cases include multiple fractures at different stages of healing, multiple rib fractures, and stories inconsistent with the patient's age, like an 8-month-old jumping on the bed. Physicians and providers are trained to look for patterns of abuse and are required to report them by law, which means we are mandatory reporters. We are required to err on the side of child safety, and this does not necessarily mean a parent is being accused of wrongdoing.

In many states, teachers are mandatory reporters. In some states, all persons over the age of 18 are mandatory reporters while the other states allow for "permissive reporting," which means you can report suspicions to authorities without fear of retaliation. The reason we work so hard to report these cases is that historically 5-10% of missed abuse cases can result in death at a later time from repeat abuse. It can actually mean the life of a child, which makes it a high priority for physicians.

In the case that you suspect child abuse has occurred to your child, you should *always* seek care for your child. Perhaps you're concerned the child was injured by another adult when at a day care or by your spouse. Perhaps you may have injured your child accidentally. Perhaps you know your child was injured by your significant other, but you are scared of retaliation if you take your child in to be seen. Do not be afraid to seek appropriate medical care for your child out of fear of being blamed or losing your child. Your child's health matters first and foremost. Likewise, such situations do not automatically mean you will be separated from your child, and resources are available if you are concerned about retaliation from a known abuser.

If you are in immediate danger at any point, contact EMS at 911. You can also call the National Domestic Violence Hotline at 1-800-799-7233 for assistance. There is a website called *Childhelp* that deals with child abuse. You can report suspected cases, live chat with a counselor, and find other resources for help. Their website is located at: https://www.childhelphotline.org/. You can also call or text them at 1-800-4-A-Child or 1-800-422-4453. They even have instructions on how to hide your internet history so that no one knows you have visited their website.[10]

* * *

References

1. Turner TL, Palamountain S. Patient Education: Colic (excessive crying) in infants (Beyond the Basics). UpToDate. Updated August 2024. Accessed September 3, 2024. https://www.uptodate.com/contents/colic-excessive-crying-in-infants-beyond-the-basics?source=related_link

2. How to cope and keep calm with a crying baby. National Childbirth Trust (NCT). Updated March 2022. Accessed September 3, 2024. https://www.nct.org.uk/baby-toddler/crying/how-cope-and-keep-calm-crying-baby#:~:text=How%20to%20cope%20and%20keep%20calm%20with%20a,Your%20network%20is%20broader%20than%20you%20think%20

3. Parlakian R, MacLaughlin S. How to Stay Calm When Baby Won't Stop Crying. Zero to Three. Updated February 18, 2018. Accessed September 3, 2024. https://www.zerotothree.org/resource/how-to-stay-calm-when-baby-wont-stop-crying/

4. Ranade SC, Allen AK, Deutsch SA. The Role of the Orthopaedic Surgeon in the Identification and Management of Nonaccidental Trauma. *J Am Acad Orthop Surg*. Jan 15 2020;28(2):53-65. doi:10.5435/JAAOS-D-18-00348

5. Risk and Protective Factors. Center for Disease Control: Child Abuse and Neglect Prevention. Updated May 16, 2024. Accessed September 3, 2024. https://www.cdc.gov/child-abuse-neglect/risk-factors/?CDC_AAref_Val=https://www.cdc.gov/violenceprevention/childabuseandneglect/riskprotectivefactors.html

6. Legano LA, Desch LW, Messner SA, et al. Maltreatment of Children With Disabilities. *Pediatrics*. May 2021;147(5)doi:10.1542/peds.2021-050920

7. Number of child abuse victims in the United States in 2022, by perpetrator relationship. Statista. Updated July 5, 2024. Accessed September 3, 2024. https://www.statista.com/statistics/254893/child-abuse-in-the-us-by-perpetrator-relationship/

8. Schnitzer PG, Ewigman BG. Child deaths resulting from

inflicted injuries: household risk factors and perpetrator characteristics. *Pediatrics*. Nov 2005;116(5):e687-93. doi:10.1542/peds.2005-0296

9. Zuravin SJ. Unplanned childbearing and family size: their relationship to child neglect and abuse. *Fam Plann Perspect*. Jul-Aug 1991;23(4):155-61.

10. Childhelp Our Story. Childhelp. Accessed September, 2024. https://www.childhelphotline.org/our-story/

Chapter 15
Suicide

This one is difficult to discuss. It is one of the saddest things about our society that some children and adolescents commit suicide. I'm sure all of us remember the awkward ages of being a teenager, of being unsure of the future, and of lacking confidence in ourselves or our body image, and the pressure is higher now more than ever. The number of suicides remains fairly consistent with time, not increasing or decreasing. Though the scope of this book is mainly targeted at children ages zero to ten, suicide is such an important topic for adolescents and teenagers that it's worth including.

The checklist:

1. Identify children at higher risk and get help
2. Restrict access to firearms and medications

Though it is certainly morbid to discuss, suicide was the **NUMBER ONE** overall cause of death in children ages 10-14 from physical harm rather than medical issue. This is more toward the side of 13 and 14 rather than 10 and 11 because that's when puberty hits and adolescent emotion runs high. Compared to the other causes of death on our lists, this one is intentional and self-inflicted. In other words, all the other causes we've discussed are things you can accidentally do to your child or they can accidentally do to themselves due to being incapable of caring for themselves reasonably. This is the first age group where your child becomes more of a danger to themselves on their own power.

As far as prevention, I will not claim to be an expert, nor do I have teenagers at this point in my life from whom to draw personal experience. Therefore, I have heavily relied on the research of others to support this chapter. The CDC highlights both the risk factors and the protective factors and these are listed below.[1] These are divided into individual, relationship, community, and societal. Monitor your child for these risk factors. You should be wary of children/adolescents who seem to show extremes of emotion like anxiety or rage or express feelings of hopelessness or say they want to die or feel guilty. If you notice these trends in your child, *talk* to them and research resources on how to help them, such as a counselor. Schools provide counselors, and there are many religion-based counselors available that try to provide aid even to those with limited financial means.

Individual Risk Factors

- Previous suicide attempt
- History of depression and other mental illnesses
- Serious illness such as chronic pain
- Criminal/legal problems
- Job/financial problems or loss
- Impulsive or aggressive tendencies
- Substance use
- Current or prior history of adverse childhood experiences
- Sense of hopelessness

- Violence victimization and/or perpetration

Relationship Risk Factors

- Bullying
- Family/loved one's history of suicide
- Loss of relationships
- High conflict or violent relationships
- Social isolation

Community Risk Factors

- Lack of access to healthcare
- Suicide cluster in the community
- Stress of acculturation
- Community violence
- Historical trauma
- Discrimination

Societal Risk Factors

- Stigma associated with help-seeking and mental illness
- Easy access to lethal means of suicide among people at risk
- Unsafe media portrayals of suicide

There have been recent concerns that the media has glamorized suicide. There was a show called *13 Reasons Why* first released in 2017 based off of a book. The show is about a girl who commits suicide and provides tapes she records prior to her death that tell the story of why she decides to commit suicide. I myself have never watched the show. Controversies arose because some alarm bells went off after the show was released. In children aged 10 to 17, the overall suicide rate rose by 29% in the month after the first season was released, though mostly males were affected.[2] The show also gained criticism for portraying mental healthcare resources as not helpful and maybe depicting them in a negative light.[3] Some adolescents showed a worsening mood (23.7%) after watching the show in a study using anonymous surveys.[4] Regardless, the main point is that books, television, and movies can affect the way your child might view themselves. Maintaining open communication about the content your child consumes may help with navigating how these portrayals affect their developing thought processes.

Warning Signs

According to the Mayo Clinic, the warning signs that a teen might be suicidal include: talking or writing about suicide, using increasing amounts of alcohol or drugs, feeling trapped or hopeless, doing risky or self-destructive things, and giving away personal items for no logical reason.[5] They also include a teen changing their normal routine such as eating or sleeping patterns, becoming less social and wanting to be alone, and having mood swings. If you notice the above in any of your children, get help. One service that's available 24/7 is called the 988 Suicide and Crisis Lifeline. Send a text to the number 988 to initiate a conversation.

Mental health conditions such as depression and anxiety are medical conditions that can be treated. If you suspect your child is suffering from one of these conditions, seek medical care. Sometimes there can be shame associated with seeing a mental health professional, but it is important to destigmatize this. Parents should err on the side of getting their kids help rather than putting aside concerns and not taking them seriously.

By the Numbers

Since this is a book about prevention, I will discuss the statistics on successful suicide attempts. Many more people attempt suicide than are successful. The Youth Risk Behavior Surveillance System (YRBSS) is a set of surveys sent out every other year since 1991 to many high schools and some middle schools. Over 10,000 students respond on average.. The surveys cover multiple topics, such as sexual activity, substance abuse, and suicide among others. The Youth Risk Behavior Survey (YRBS) reports the actual data, similar to WISQARS.

YRBS data reports the percentage of high school students who felt sad or hopeless at any time within the 12 months prior to answering the survey was 29.9% in 2013, 36.7% in 2019, and 42.3% in 2021, the most recent year available at the time of writing this book. There is a disturbing trend upward.

The number of high school students who seriously considered attempting suicide was 18.8% in 2019 and 22.2% in 2021.

The number who made a plan about how they would attempt suicide was: 15.7% in 2019 and 2021.

The number who actually attempted suicide was 8.9% in 2019 and 10.2% in 2021.

The number whose suicide attempt resulted in treatment by a doctor or nurse was 2.5% in 2019 and 2.9% in 2021.

The data show an increase in 2021, which was likely affected by COVID and COVID lockdowns.[7] Surveys are not perfect data because not everyone responds to them, but they are still the best data available. The big point here is that a large number of adolescents at least consider suicide, and even up to 10% attempt suicide. That is one in every ten adolescents surveyed, and that is a sobering statistic.

Mechanisms of Suicide

According to WISQARS in 2019, in children ages 10-14 who committed suicide, suffocation was the number one killer at 317 deaths (59.4% of all suicides), followed by firearms at 172 (32.2%) and poisoning (i.e. intentional overdose of medications) at 30 deaths (5.6%). Suffocation in this case usually means hanging. In children ages 15-19, firearms were the leading cause of successful suicide at 995 deaths (45%) followed by 852 deaths by suffocation (38.6%). The third-place cause was poisoning with 177 deaths (8%).

As for firearms, if you think your child is at risk, *restrict* their access to firearms. In fact, restrict access to *all* children. Firearms are overall the number one reason for successful suicide attempts, especially in adults compared to hanging or other means. According to the AAP Advocacy statement on suicide, 91% of all suicide attempts with firearms are successful versus 23% success rate with intentional drug overdose.[8] Higher death rates from hanging in adolescents compared to firearm use is likely due to less opportunity for adolescents and younger teenagers to obtain firearms compared with older teenagers and adults because they cannot legally purchase them. As with the prior chapter on firearm safety (Chapter 12), use locked safes if you own firearms, and do not let your child have the code. Suicide attempts with firearms are quicker and more susceptible to impulsive behavior because you only have to pull a trigger. Suffocation takes a lot more effort, and intentional medication overdose and self-inflicted cutting take more time, which allows opportunity to abandon the attempt.

A Word on Social Media

I believe social media has a role in our society that can be negative at times. One of the downsides of social media is its potential to draw attention to the events that your child may not be getting invited to. They may see pictures of their friends or acquaintances at parties or going on trips together that may have gone unnoticed prior to the era of social media. Likewise, many on social media portray their lives in a way that makes their life seem more grandiose than it may be. You can make your life into a highlight reel and display for all to see, and some children may either be envious or feel as though something is missing or wrong with their life because they don't have as much fun as others appear to have on social media. Cyberbullying is certainly a factor because it allows people to anonymously say vicious things to one another that they would have never said to someone's face.

Social media is ubiquitous in our society at this point. The American Psychological Association has a panel on social media that released an update in May of 2023, but it is very vague with respect to appropriate ages for social media use.[9] Dr. Mitch Prinstein, who is the APA's chief science offer has been quoted saying "I certainly don't think anyone under 13 should be using it.[10]" He also added "Unfettered access, without any screen controls or monitoring, that should probably be delayed for as long as possible – certainly, until at least 16." I agree with him, but I'm not an expert on psychiatry. Some major tech developers and moguls don't even let their own children use it.[11]

This is pure speculation on my part, but my concern is that it can alter perceptions of reality and cause more concern for stress in a youngster's mind. I would try to encourage other activities over social media and to make sure adolescents and teenagers know social media is not a substitute for interactions in real life. Children may get a dopamine addiction when it comes to getting "likes" on social media posts and try to be as outrageous as possible in order to get attention. They may mistake social media "likes" as real affection and put too much effort into getting "likes" rather than finding true companionship. As with pretty much everything in life, things can be good in moderation but not with excess. One study found a time dependent risk for depression in teens that use social media, meaning it worsened with more time spent on social media.[12] The risk reportedly increased by 13% for each hour increase in social media use and was a stronger risk in girls than in boys. Make sure your children know the balance and try to pay attention if your adolescent or teenager is spending too much time on social media quietly.

Summary

The summary of the topic of suicide is this: talk to your child regularly and monitor for risk factors, restrict access to firearms (especially for impulsive adolescents), and seek help if you notice signs of your child withdrawing or think your child may be at risk. There are many people who think about suicide and may even reach the planning stage but do not actually perform the act. If they have easier access to something like a firearm, which makes the process quick and easy, then it's all the more dangerous because it can happen on an impulse. It takes almost no planning and does not allow them time to think through their decision while trying to harm themselves.

* * *

References

1. Risk and Protective Factors for Suicide. Center for Disease Control: Suicide Prevention. Updated April 25, 2024. Accessed September 3, 2024. https://www.cdc.gov/suicide/risk-factors/?CDC_AAref_Val=https://www.cdc.gov/suicide/factors/index.html

2. Bridge JA, Greenhouse JB, Ruch D, et al. Association Between the Release of Netflix's 13 Reasons Why and Suicide Rates in the United States: An Interrupted Time Series Analysis. *J Am Acad Child Adolesc Psychiatry*. Feb 2020;59(2):236-243. doi:10.1016/j.jaac.2019.04.020

3. SCCAP Statement on 13 Reasons Why. The Society of Clinical Child and Adolescent Psychology. Updated May 4, 2017. Accessed September 3, 2024. https://web.archive.org/web/

20170622051137/https:/clinicalchildpsychology.org/sccap-statement-13-reasons-why

4. Rosa GSD, Andrades GS, Caye A, Hidalgo MP, Oliveira MAB, Pilz LK. Thirteen Reasons Why: The impact of suicide portrayal on adolescents' mental health. *J Psychiatr Res*. Jan 2019;108:2-6. doi:10.1016/j.jpsychires.2018.10.018

5. Tween and teen health. The Mayo Clinic. Accessed September 3, 2024. https://www.mayoclinic.org/healthy-lifestyle/tween-and-teen-health/in-depth/teen-suicide/art-20044308

6. Brener N, Kann L, Shanklin S, et al. Methodology of the Youth Risk Behavior Surveillance System - 2013. Centers for Disease Control: Morbidity and Mortality Weekly Report. Updated March 1, 2013. Accessed September 3, 2024.

7. YRBSS Results. Center for Disease Control: Youth Risk Behavior Surveillance System (YRBSS). Updated June 14, 2024. Accessed September 3, 2024. https://www.cdc.gov/yrbs/results/index.html

8. Safe Storage of Firearms. American Academy of Pediatrics: Advocacy. Updated January 26, 2024. Accessed September 3, 2024. https://www.aap.org/en/advocacy/state-advocacy/safe-storage-of-firearms/#:~:text=Suicide%20attempts%20involving%20a%20-firearm%20more%20often%20are%20fatal

9. Health Advisory on Social Media Use in Adolescence. American Psychological Association. Updated May 2023. Accessed September 25, 2024. https://www.apa.org/topics/social-media-internet/health-advisory-adolescent-social-media-use

10. Huddleston T. Is there a 'right' age for kids to be on social media? 'I certainly don't think anyone under 13' should use it, expert says. CNBC. Updated May 26, 2023. Accessed September 3, 2024. https://www.cnbc.com/2023/05/26/the-right-age-for-kids-to-be-on-social-media-experts-say.html

11. Rudgard O. The tech moguls who invented social media have banned their children from it. Irish Independent. Updated November 5, 2018. Accessed September 3, 2024. https://www.inde

pendent.ie/life/family/parenting/the-tech-moguls-who-invented-social-media-have-banned-their-children-from-it/37494367.html

12. Liu M, Kamper-DeMarco KE, Zhang J, Xiao J, Dong D, Xue P. Time Spent on Social Media and Risk of Depression in Adolescents: A Dose-Response Meta-Analysis. *Int J Environ Res Public Health*. Apr 24 2022;19(9)doi:10.3390/ijerph19095164

Chapter 16

Traumatic Brain Injury and Spinal Cord Injury

What about other serious risks to your child? Death is certainly terrible, but death isn't the only terrible outcome for an injury. Permanent impairment to limb or brain is another terrible fate. In this chapter, I will explain what traumatic brain injury (TBI) and spinal cord injury (SCI) are and who is at risk with what activities. I think the general public is relatively uninformed on these topics, so I will try to give an easy-to-understand background to reduce confusion. Then we will discuss the statistics and potential for prevention.

Warning: the following paragraphs contain background information, feel free to skip to page 178 if you find it boring and don't care to know the details

The brain and spinal cord are both part of what we call the central nervous system. The nervous system is the organ of the body responsible for both voluntary and involuntary (or automatic) control for all the actions of our body, including most of the other organs (digestive system, urinary system, etc.). The nervous system is split into the central nervous system and the peripheral nervous system. The central nervous system includes the brain and spinal cord, and the peripheral nervous system includes the string-like nerves that cover every other part of our body.

The brain sits within your skull and contains many different parts that function for voluntary control (walking, talking, thinking, etc.) and also contains parts that regulate the body with involuntary control (breathing, temperature regulation, ability to balance, etc.). There is also a third part of the nervous system called the autonomic nervous system which controls automatic functions, such as the process of your stomach digesting food and passing it on throughout the rest of your intestines, or your ability to sweat, or your body's ability to regulate blood pressure and control which organs receive more blood depending on the state of your body and circumstances (fight or flight response, if you will). The brain needs a way to send signals downward to the rest of the body, and this is accomplished by the spinal cord.

The spinal cord is a bundle of nerves that travels as a unit from the bottom of the brain down the spine. It is enveloped by the bony spine, which has 31 vertebral block units that act as a protective shield. The spinal cord travels down through a tunnel that is covered with bone to protect the precious cord, and it gives off nerves at every level to give the ability to feel as well as the ability to move and react. These nerves are called peripheral nerves, and they are arranged systematically from head to toe. The brain and spinal cord are surrounded by fluid called cerebrospinal fluid. The fluid is clear, and it serves as a cushion to these structures and provides nutrients. For women who've had an epidural during childbirth, this involves sticking a needle between one of the gaps in the vertebral bone column to inject medicine into the space surrounding the spinal cord to numb it.

Nerves are one of the tissues in our bodies with the least regenerative potential. If you scrape your skin, it can heal, and new skin cells are created. Nerve cells cannot be regrown if they completely die. If they are severed, they can recover through a healing process, but this process can be painstakingly slow.

Newborns are born with more nerve cells in their brains than we have as adults, and they slowly prune or discard the ones they don't use over time. So why are adults more intelligent than infants if we have fewer brain cells? As we develop, our brain cells make connections to one another and refine those connections so that they become natural and efficient. So, our brain cells are wired in a more complex system to function efficiently whereas an infant's brain contains mostly fresh nerve cells without many connections. You memorized a poem during second grade and can still remember it? That's because nerves in your brain created a connection after repetition that you still have to this day, although you might not remember it as well if you haven't practiced lately and refreshed that connection.

Now that the "boring" stuff is out of the way:

Traumatic brain injury (TBI) is defined as any injury to the brain resulting from a trauma, regardless of how big or small the trauma. These injuries can range from very mild with full recovery up to death, whether immediate or delayed. Aside from death from TBI, the most significant brain injury is one that results in permanent impairment. More severe injuries may not result in death but may cause permanent mental and/or physical disability. The bad news is 475,000 children are estimated to sustain TBI yearly in the U.S., and 5,000 of these result in disability.[1] One study reports motor vehicle crashes are the most common cause of hospitalization for TBI at 38.9% followed by falls at 21.2%.[2] This study, however, included any person aged 20 or under as a "child." Adolescents ages 15 and above have higher risk of severe TBI, particularly males, so these numbers may be skewed compared to my target discussion point of ages 10 and below. If a child under the age of 2 suffers a TBI, it is most likely to be due to child abuse, estimated at 53% in one study.[3] In a study that reviewed data from 2000 to 2002, reportedly 98% of children had a normal Glasgow Coma Score during ER evaluation for TBI, which is a score that looks at brain function based on a quick examination of the patient.[4] This is the good news: the vast majority of children evaluated at the hospital for head injury only have minor injuries with full recovery, and this does not include children who did not even come into the hospital, so the overall chances of a significant brain injury are less than 2%.

If you decide to do your own research on TBI, keep in mind that it can be confusing how deaths and disability are counted. Most deaths in a motor vehicle crash technically occur due to terminal brain injury, so deaths can be double counted as both a motor vehicle death and a TBI death depending on the resource. The same can be true for spinal cord injury. High speed motor vehicle crashes often result in the skull becoming internally detached from the spine, which severs the spinal cord right at the top, which causes instant death. It's more of a question of technicality. Studies reporting these topics may differ in how the actual "cause" of death is reported.

Types of Traumatic Brain Injury

There are multiple types of TBI, including diffuse injuries, or injury to the entire brain, and focal injuries, or an injury to specific areas of the brain.[5] The specifics probably are not necessary for this discussion, but the most common type of TBI is concussion, which is best thought of as a brain bruise. This either comes from direct contact to the head or indirect contact through whiplash type injury, in which rapid motion of the head will cause the brain to contact the inside of the skull. The brain can also sustain injuries to its surrounding blood supply, or hematomas, which are bleeding pockets that swell that can begin to push on the brain. Some hematomas require emergent surgical drilling by a neurosurgeon to relieve pressure or else the brain can be compressed too much and cause death.

Treatment for Traumatic Brain Injury

TBIs are treated in a number of ways, the most common of which is observation or a period of monitoring. Certain TBIs require surgical intervention or invasive monitoring, which requires surgically inserting a monitor to measure the pressure within the brain and the surrounding fluid or the chemical properties of the fluid itself along with the chemistry of the blood. The biggest risk with severe TBI is swelling. The brain swells just like any other body part when injured, and the more severe the swelling, the higher the risk of permanent or deadly injury to the brain.

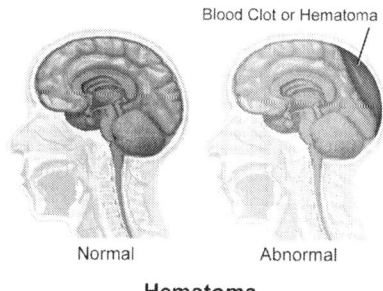

Hematoma

Image credit BruceBlaus under the license Creative Commons Attribution-Share Alike 4.0 International, Image link: https://commons.wikimedia.org/wiki/File:Hematoma_Comparison.png, license link: https://creativecommons.org/licenses/by-sa/4.0/

In fact, most medical treatments for severe TBI are geared at either preventing swelling or trying to monitor for progression of swelling.

The skull is a wonderful protector of the brain because it is a hard surface, but it also is a hard enclosed box that does not allow much room for swelling. The exception is with younger children because the skull has not fully closed at birth, which allows the child's head to be soft and pass through the birth canal. (However, you should always seek help from a medical provider if you believe your newborn has sustained a head injury!) By the time you are older, however, the skull does not allow swelling, which is a dangerous risk for a brain that has been injured. As the brain swells, the pressure inside the skull increases dramatically, cutting off circulation and oxygen to the brain. This can result in permanent damage or death. Other problems with TBI include body temperature control because the regulatory center for your body temperature is within the brain. With loss of temperature regulation, the body may require heating or cooling from an outside source to keep the body temperature within its functional range. This is usually performed in an intensive care unit (ICU). Otherwise, your body may heat or cool itself to extreme temperatures that can lead to injury and death. Hopefully this gives you an entry level understanding of what TBI is and a basic idea of how it is treated.

Spinal Cord Injury

This section is background, so feel free to skip if you find it boring.

Spinal cord injury (SCI) can occur multiple ways, but most often it is from some sort of severe bending motion in the spine that breaks the stability of the spinal column. The spinal cord can then stretch more than it's supposed to (nerves hate stretching), and the bony parts of the spine can also shift and squish the spinal cord. Imagine a pool noodle with the hole down its center. Now imagine inserting a wooden broom stick through that hole so you have wood surrounded by pool noodle. Now make that inverse. Pretend you have a wooden pool noodle with the spongy material now in the center. Pretend that spongy material is vitally important and cannot be hit or cut or stretched or punched. The real spinal column has spaces at different levels to allow nerves to exit and allow your torso and neck to bend but keep this pool noodle example as a crude reference. If something were to break the wooden outer shell into two pieces, the pieces could go back and forth in any direction and the spongy central material would be stretched and squished or potentially even completely severed in half. This is how many spinal cord injuries occur. The bony spine and/or its supporting ligaments are disrupted, allowing too much motion and therefore the spinal cord gets kinked. The most common offenders are car or motorcycle wrecks and gunshot wounds that pass through the spinal column.

We grade spinal cord injuries on the American Spinal Injury Association (ASIA) scale.[6] The most important part of this classification that lets us know the severity of the injury is whether *anything* nerve related works below the level of the spinal cord injury. We test the nerve function in the lowest levels of the spinal cord to see if any function remains. If there is no function, the injury is "complete" and the injured level and below will never regain function. If there is any sort of preservation of function (even if it's just sensation without movement), there's a chance for recovery because nerve function is still present. With "incomplete" injuries, the quicker someone regains function in the hours, days, and weeks after the injury, the better their chance for recovery. The better the amount of function initially after the injury (being able to still move the legs but weakly, for example) also predicts better return of function. Sometimes the injury is *incomplete* but still so severe that it does not recover much at all. For example, someone with sensation of the legs but no ability to move would have an *incomplete* injury.

The spine has a systematic organization that follows the function of the body. The spine contains multiple vertebra (33 to be exact), and we break these down into sections: cervical, thoracic, lumbar, sacral, and coccygeal. Vertebrae (singular vertebra) are the block-like bones that make up your spine. The cervical, thoracic, and lumbar vertebrae are the mobile vertebrae that make up the spine, while the sacrum and coccyx consist of fused vertebrae that are essentially a singular block that move as a unit. The cervical vertebrae are the 7 bones that make up the neck, the thoracic vertebrae are the 12 bones that make up the spine that connects to the ribcage below the neck, and the 5 lumbar vertebrae (i.e. the lower back) are between the rib cage and the pelvis.

Jordan Paynter, MD

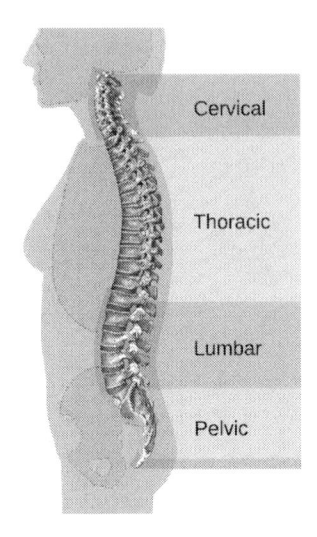

Image credit Vsion and Jmarchn under the license Creative Commons Attribution-Share Alike 4.0 International, Image link: https://commons.wikimedia.org/wiki/File:Spinal_column_curvature-en.svg , license link: https://creativecommons.org/licenses/by-sa/4.0/

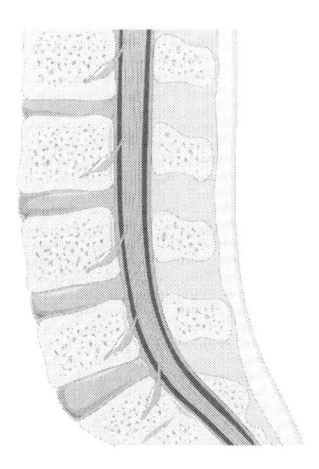

Image credit Laboratoires Servier SMARt-Servier Medical Art under the license Creative Commons Attribution-Share Alike 3.0 Unported, Image link: https://commons.wikimedia.org/wiki/File:Spine_-_Vertebral_column_4_--_Smart-Servier.png , license link: https://creativecommons.org/licenses/by-sa/3.0/

Using complete SCI as an example, the higher up you have an injury, the more severe problems and the more disability. Injury at the cervical, or neck, level will result in loss of the use of the legs, the muscles of the thorax, and either some or all of the arm muscles. The level of the injury means the location of the injury, so a high level would be toward the neck, and a low level would be toward the buttocks. High injuries at the third cervical vertebrae or above require permanent ventilator assistance for breathing due to loss of the use of the muscles that allow the lungs to expand. Complete injuries at the thoracic level do not allow use of the legs whereas lumbar levels may allow some use of the legs depending on the level. Both thoracic and lumbar level injuries allow use of the arms and at least some of the breathing muscles. Incomplete injuries at any level may allow some use of the limbs below the level of the injury as well as the chance of recovery with time. Hopefully this demystifies a little bit of what spinal cord injury is and what the recovery can look like.

Children and Spinal Cord Injury

Children are relatively protected from SCI overall relative to adults because of the flexibility of the spine and the potential for recovery. The most common causes of cervical spine injury in younger children include motor vehicle collision and falls from heights, particularly more than 10 feet. Diving is a risk for teenagers. Sports can also be a cause of injury, particularly in children older than eight.[7] Children younger than 8 are at relatively higher risk of upper cervical spine injury between the base of the skull and the second cervical vertebra compared to older children and adults. This is partly due to the anatomy of the joints in the vertebra, the relatively larger head size of younger children, and the extra flexibility of the surrounding soft tissues in the cervical spine.

The best thing you can do as a non-medical provider if you suspect a spine injury has occurred is to not move the child. Let trained medical professionals move someone because sometimes the spine may have broken but not injured the spinal cord within, but a rapid or bending movement to the unstable spine could pinch or damage the cord and cause injury. Therefore, the victim may not yet have permanent damage but could become injured or even paralyzed from improper movement.

The good news is that permanent spinal cord injuries in children are relatively rare. The following data are pulled from the National Spinal Cord Injury Statistical Center (NSCISC) public database from the year 2016[8], which is published by the University of Alabama at Birmingham. The data I reviewed includes approximately 32,000 people between 1972-2016. In this database over that time period of 44 years, only 196 of the injuries occurred in children less than age 10, accounting for only 0.61% of the database. Expanding up to age 16 increases the percentage to 5.51%. According to the 2016 database study, 48.2% of all SCI occur between the ages of 16 and 30. When you consider children less than 10, it is a relatively rare event, and that should reassure you.

Hopefully you feel slightly more educated on what traumatic brain injury and spinal cord injury are. I know I've discussed some scary things here, but hopefully the other thing you take away is that it is rare for children to have permanent disability from these injuries. This is meant to show you that though bad things certainly can happen, children are very capable of resisting injury and do well. Older teenagers are more of a problem to themselves, particularly males, but this is outside the scope of this book. If you stick to the prior sections on how to prevent the major injuries: taking time to make sure your child is appropriately secured in the appropriate car seat every time you place them in a vehicle, avoiding higher risk activities, wearing helmets during appropriate activities, the chances are relatively low of either of these issues occurring.

* * *

References

1. Vavilala M, Tasker R. Severe traumatic brain injury (TBI) in children: Initial evaluation and management. UpToDate. Updated August 2024. Accessed September 3, 2024. https://www.uptodate.com/contents/severe-traumatic-brain-injury-tbi-in-children-initial-evaluation-and-management?search=tbi%20children&source=search_result&selectedTitle=1~150&usage_type=default&display_rank=1

2. Shi J, Xiang H, Wheeler K, et al. Costs, mortality likelihood and outcomes of hospitalized US children with traumatic brain injuries. *Brain Inj*. Jul 2009;23(7):602-11. doi:10.1080/02699050903014907

3. Keenan HT, Runyan DK, Marshall SW, Nocera MA, Merten DF, Sinal SH. A population-based study of inflicted traumatic brain injury in young children. *JAMA*. Aug 6 2003;290(5):621-6. doi:10.1001/jama.290.5.621

4. Dunning J, Daly JP, Malhotra R, et al. The implications of NICE guidelines on the management of children presenting with head injury. *Arch Dis Child*. Aug 2004;89(8):763-7. doi:10.1136/adc.2003.042523

5. Araki T, Yokota H, Morita A. Pediatric Traumatic Brain Injury: Characteristic Features, Diagnosis, and Management. *Neurol Med Chir (Tokyo)*. Feb 15 2017;57(2):82-93. doi:10.2176/nmc.ra.2016-0191

6. International Standards for Nerological Classification of Spinal Cord Injury (ISNCSCI). American Spinal Injury Association (ASIA). Accessed September 3, 2024. https://www.asia-spinalinjury.org/wp-content/uploads/2019/10/ASIA-ISCOS-Worksheet_10.2019_PRINT-Page-1-2.pdf

7. Leonard J. Evaluation and acute management of cervical spine injuries in children and adolescents. UpToDate. Updated August 8, 2024. Accessed September 3, 2024. https://www.uptodate.com/contents/evaluation-and-acute-management-of-cervical-spine-

injuries-in-children-and-adolescents?topicRef=15603&source=related_link

8. 2016 Annual Report - Public Version. National Spinal Cord Injury Statistical Center (NSCISC). Accessed September 3, 2024. https://www.nscisc.uab.edu/Public/2016%20Annual%20Report%20-%20Complete%20Public%20Version.pdf

Chapter 17

Lightning Strikes

The next two chapters focus on topics that we hear about because of media exposure or natural senses of danger. In this chapter I will discuss lightning, and in the next chapter I will discuss animal attacks. Fortunately, deaths in all age groups, especially children, are rare from these events, but I thought it would be a worthwhile inclusion because of the innate concerns many parents have over such events.

Though lightning strikes are often feared by parents, fortunately, they are rare. According to the National Weather Service, the average yearly death toll from lightning strikes from all ages was 27 from 2009-2018.[1] Lightning strikes accounted for an estimated 243 injuries per year. Therefore, only 10% of those struck are killed. This includes all ages. The number of deaths of children is fewer.

Common outdoor recreational and work activities place people at higher risk. This includes fishing, boating, sports and sitting on the beach. Farmers are the workers at highest risk for lightning strikes while on the job.

Lightning probably gets a lot of attention because it's loud and usually obvious when it's a danger, though not always. The threat of a lightning strike is often more dangerous at the beginning of a storm before nearby people are aware that the oncoming storm can produce lightning. However, there are an estimated 25 million lightning strikes yearly in the US, so lightning injuries are relatively rare considering the circumstances.[2] At 243 total injuries from 25 million strikes, that's a 0.00000972% chance of being hit.

Lightning (and electrocution in general) harms the body in multiple ways. The direct effect of the electrical current can overpower the heart's natural pacing rhythm and cause the heart muscle to change from a steady, controlled pace to a chaotic and uncoordinated firing. When the muscles of the heart do not work in coordination, the heart cannot effectively pump blood throughout the body. Alternatively, the heart may stop pumping altogether after a strike. Electrical shock can also directly damage other tissues of the body from heat generated by the current. Cells of the body can also be disrupted by the electrical charge itself. Lastly, victims often go into a spasm and lose control of their body temporarily and can fall.[2]

Prevention

For prevention of lightning strikes, the best practice is to always seek shelter indoors when you hear thunder. Check local weather alerts when playing outside during high-risk times of the year such as spring or summer. The American Red Cross recommends avoiding devices connected to electrical outlets during a thunderstorm as well as avoiding running water because lightning can travel through the water lines.[3] The CDC echoes the same situations and includes washing dishes and bathing.[4] They elaborate on devices connected to electrical outlets to include computers, laptops, game systems, dyers, or electric stoves. Avoid windows, doors, and porches. Do not lie or lean on concrete floors or walls because the lightning can travel through the metal reinforcement bars that are present within these structures. Do not use a corded phone, either. (Does anyone still do that?)

Bare Bones

The CDC also has many recommendations for when you cannot get indoors quickly, which I have adapted into this paragraph.[4] If you are outdoors and cannot get to shelter immediately, theoretically you can reduce your chances of being struck by crouching down in a ball-like position with your head tucked and hands over your ears. You should not lie flat. Lying down increases the surface area of your body in contact with the ground and can make you more likely to suffer more severe injury if struck. Do not stand near a lone tree or telephone pole. Lightning tends to strike taller structures. Stick to lower trees if you are caught in a forest. Get away from bodies of water such as ponds or lakes, and stay away from metal wires or powerlines that can conduct electricity. If you are in a group, separate from one another to reduce the number of injuries if lightning strikes. If you are in a boat and there is even a threat of lightning, immediately go to shore. Try to stay away from open fields or playgrounds. In the event you witness a lightning strike, call 911. If the victim is unresponsive, begin CPR immediately.

* * *

References

1. How Dangerous is Lightning? National Weather Service. Accessed September 3, 2024. https://www.weather.gov/safety/lightning-odds

2. O'Keefe K. Electrical injuries and lightning strikes: Evaluation and management. UpToDate. Updated August 2024. Accessed September 3, 2024. https://www.uptodate.com/contents/electrical-injuries-and-lightning-strikes-evaluation-and-management?search=lightning%20strike&source=search_result&selectedTitle=1%7E71&usage_type=default&display_rank=1

3. Thunderstorm Preparedness Checklist. American Red Cross. Updated November 1, 2022. Accessed September 3, 2024. https://www.redcross.org/content/dam/redcross/atg/PDF_s/Prepared

ness___Disaster_Recovery/Disaster_Preparedness/Thunderstorm/Thunderstorm.pdf

    4.Safety Guidelines: Lightning. Center for Disease Control: Lightning. Updated April 15, 2024. Accessed September 3, 2024. https://www.cdc.gov/lightning/safety/?CDC_AAref_Val=https://www.cdc.gov/disasters/lightning/safetytips.html

Chapter 18

Animals and Allergies

This chapter is dedicated to animals, including large animals as well as insects and arachnids. They are not a particularly common source of death in children, but I believe there's a lot of fear around specific animals, including snakes and sharks because of the publicity that surrounds such attacks and deaths. Which living creatures are the biggest threat to you and your children? Let's find out.

Quiz time, what non-human animal is responsible for the most deaths in the United States per year? The answer is deer. This is technically an indirect effect because the vast majority of deaths caused by deer are from vehicle crashes either into a deer or as a result of swerving to avoid a deer. One paper estimates up to 440 yearly deaths from deer, with some others estimating between 100-200 per year.[1] Interestingly, it seems driving in West Virginia carries the highest risk. This ultimately goes back to the chapter on vehicle safety: remember to buckle your children appropriately in the car!

The animals most likely to cause death as a result of direct attack are:

1. Farm animals such as horses and cows (72 per year)
2. Hornets, wasps, and bees (60 per year)
3. Dogs (34 per year)
4. Venomous snakes and lizard (6 per year)
5. Venomous spiders (6 per year)

This is according to a study reviewing animal fatalities in the US from 2008-2015.[2] This data includes all ages, not just children.

Farm Animals

Farm animals such as cows and horses are larger mammals and can either throw a human off when riding, kick them, or trample them accidentally. Such events can also result in severe brain injury or spinal cord injury. There was a large horse-riding population near where I trained in residency, and in March or April of every year, horse injuries started to increase because of the improving weather. I helped treat multiple patients who sustained spinal cord injuries from riding horses.

Dogs

Dogs are, of course, man's best friend, but there are so many domestic dogs in the U.S. (89.7 million estimated in 2017) that it's honestly surprising there aren't more accidental deaths.[3] Of particular importance, children under the age of four are at the highest risk for dog-related deaths. The rate is estimated 4.6 deaths per 10 million persons.[4] Keep in mind that not all dogs are harmless and to be especially careful when you are introducing dogs to young children they have not met before.

Sharks and Crocodiles

Sharks and crocodiles seem to invoke a lot of fear because of media coverage of attacks when they rarely occur. They are responsible for less than one death per year on average in the US. They make for entertaining movie plots, however.

Hornets, Wasps, Bees, and Ants

Hornets, wasps, bees, and fire ants are part of a biological order of insects called *Hymenoptera*. Most notably, they all share a similar chemical structure to their venoms, which means the effects are similar across all of this class. What's the difference between poison and venom? Venom is injected whereas poison is ingested through the oral cavity. Interestingly, there is a rating of sting potency and duration called the Schmidt Insect Sting Pain Index across the entire Hymenoptera class. It was developed by Dr. Justin Schmidt, who was an entomologist, or a scientist who studies insects and arachnids. He willingly allowed himself to be stung by dozens of different bees, wasps, hornets, and ants and rated the severity of the pain in addition to the duration of the pain. It was certainly a "dirty job," but I guess someone had to do it! If you're curious, the bullet ant is the most painful sting in the world. Dr. Schmidt described it as "pure, intense, brilliant pain. Like walking over a flaming charcoal with a 3-inch nail embedded in your heel.[5]" Notably, the pain also lasts longer than any other sting.

The bullet ant is located in in Central and South America. A native tribe in Brazil called the Sateré-Mawé uses bullet ants as part of their initiation rites for a boy to become a man. *National Geographic* once did a special covering this ritual.[6] They report that boys as young as 12 years old must stick their hands into woven gloves full of bullet ants. The ants are paralyzed in a solution and then woven into gloves with their stingers facing inward. Once the ants are awake, the participant must stick his hands in the gloves for more than ten minutes. The boy must then complete this 20 times in order to become a man and true warrior in their culture. Allegedly, the bullet ant sting is 30 times worse than that of a common honeybee. And you thought growing up in the U.S. was difficult!

I studied abroad in Costa Rica with the University of Georgia during my undergraduate education. During my tropical ecology class, one of my classmates decided he wanted to experience the sting of a bullet ant, so we caught one in the rain forest. He agitated it and allowed it to sting him. He said the worst part was the fact that the pain did not let up. He told me it hurt for at least 10 hours straight at maximum pain, and he couldn't sleep all night because of it. Fortunately, I was never stung by one.

Hymenoptera kill most often by anaphylactic reactions to the venom, especially if injected multiple times. I will explain more about the mechanism in a subsequent section and describe how it works and how to treat it.

Arachnids

Scorpions and spiders are not Hymenoptera, they are arachnids. Their venoms work differently than Hymenoptera. Scorpion stings recorded only two deaths between 2008 and 2015 in the United States.[2] Scorpions in the U.S. sting with venom that has neuromuscular toxins.[7] This affects the nervous system and muscles and can have various levels of effects ranging from local pain at the sting site up to nerve dysfunction in the face, spasms, muscle tissue death, uncontrolled salivation, and fevers. There is anti-venom available. Scorpion stings typically happen when a human accidentally steps on one or reaches under a rock or structure without looking. If you suspect a sting, visit your nearest emergency center and consider calling your state poison control center.

As for spiders, there are two species in the U.S. that pose the biggest threat: the black widow and the brown recluse. Black widow spider venom contains a neurotoxin that can lead to muscle spasms, profuse sweating, nausea, vomiting, headaches, and a fast heart rate.[8] Most bites by black widow spiders are treated with medications only and rarely require anti-venom. If a bite is suspected, you should take your child to the nearest emergency department. Medical toxicologists are available through the poison control center at 1-800-222-1222 and are often consulted by emergency medicine physicians for assistance.

The brown recluse spider is found in the South, West, and Midwest in the U.S.[9] Their venom is different from the black widow's. Brown recluse venom contains necrotizing enzymes that can directly kill tissues. The bite lesions can expand over multiple days. Symptoms can include fever, nausea and vomiting, dark urine color, and jaundice (yellowish eyes and skin). Their bites can rarely cause blood cell death, facial swelling, kidney and muscle injury and lead to coma and death. Seek attention from a medical provider if a bite is suspected.

Snakes

Snakes have been at the forefront of human-animal fear from the beginning. The serpent was the animal that seduced humanity into its fall from God in the Garden of Eden in the Bible. In the book of Genesis, when God is describing the natural curses that occur as a result of the fall of humanity, the snake is told "I will put enmity between you and the woman, and between your offspring and hers; he will crush your head, and you will strike his heel."[10], cursing humans and snakes to eternal rivalry. Regardless, snakes seem to be a common source of fear.

In the U.S., snake bites are rarely a cause of death. From 2008 to 2015, there were a total of 48 deaths, or an average of 6 per year, including adults and children.[2] There are approximately 150 species of snake in the U.S., but only four of them are venomous.[11] The four venomous species are: rattlesnakes, copperheads, cottonmouths/water moccasins, and coral snakes. Worldwide, the easiest way to determine by sight if a snake is venomous is to look at the shape of its head. Most venomous snakes have triangular shaped heads to contain their venom sacs. Nonvenomous snakes have oval shaped heads. The major exception is the coral snake, which has an oval shaped head. Thankfully, coral snakes are some of the most easily recognizable snakes by site because of their vibrant coloring. They can often be confused, however, for the king snake, which looks a lot like a coral snake. The rhyme I was taught goes, "Red and black, friend of Jack. Red and yellow, kill a fellow." This highlights the major difference in color pattern between the two snakes. The coral snake contains a yellow stripe whereas the king snake does not.

There are two major families of venomous snakes, the *Elapidae*, or elapids, and the Viperidae, or vipers. Copperheads, rattlesnakes, and cottonmouths are all vipers whereas coral snakes are elapids. Bites typically cause local skin irritation followed by swelling. Some venoms contain direct hemotoxins, or toxins that kill blood cells and damage blood vessels. They can damage tissues directly, such as the kidney or muscle. Some venom contains neurotoxins which paralyze or damage nerve endings and can prevent normal signaling pathways of the body. This prevents automatic control of organ function by the nervous system. This can lead to paralysis, coma, and death.

Not all bites from venomous snakes result in envenomation. There is a wide range of estimated rates of so called "dry bites" where venom is not injected, but the average is around 14-15%.[12] This being said, if you witness a snake bite and identify the snake as venomous, you should always assume the bite resulted in venom injection. If you cannot identify the snake, at least enough to tell it is a nonvenomous species, you should assume the bite was venomous and go to the nearest emergency medical facility.

What to Do if a Snake Bite Occurs

If a snake bite has occurred to your child, get them away from the snake as the first step. If possible, get a picture of the snake to show to a medical provider for identification.[13] Do not try to grab the snake or move it to get a better picture, as this could put you at risk of a bite. Only take a photo after you have first cared for the victim. If you grab a picture and are unsure of what type of snake you've encountered, there's a fantastic Facebook group solely dedicated to accurately identifying snakes creatively named *Snake Identification* that responds very quickly.

For the victim, cleanse the wound by rinsing with water. Immobilize the injured body part and keep it elevated to the level of the heart or below the heart, not above. Try to keep them as calm as possible so the venom does not spread. Take any jewelry or shoe wear off. Try to move the affected limb as little as possible, and try to keep the victim from trying to walk if possible.[14] Physical exertion can increase venom spread. Take your child to the nearest emergency medical facility. Call your local Poison Control Center at 1-800-222-1222 as well.

What Not To Do if a Snake Bite Occurs[15]

- Do NOT apply a tourniquet or constrictive bandage
- Do NOT slash the wound with a knife
- Do NOT suck out the venom
- Do NOT apply ice or place the injured limb in water
- Do NOT ingest caffeine as it can increase your heart rate and increase the rate of venom spread

Worldwide

Though snakebites and fatalities from snakebites are rare in the U.S., they are still common worldwide. In fact, snakes are the deadliest animal from direct attack to humans, validating their long-standing rivalry with humanity. One statistics tracker recorded 100,000 deaths by snakes worldwide in 2022 with dogs coming in second place at 30,000.[16] If you're going to be technical, mosquitos are the deadliest creature to mankind on a yearly basis because of transmissible diseases, but this is indirect.[16] The World Health Organization (WHO) states there are an estimated 5.4 million people bitten by snakes each year with 81,000 to 137,000 deaths.[17] These numbers are likely underreported because not all rural areas accurately report their numbers in the developing world.

Most of these deaths are due to lack of access to medical resources and occur in parts of India and Africa where there are many farmers that come into contact with snakes because of the nature of their work and the geographical distribution of snakes. The snakes in these parts of the world are typically more potent to begin with, but if a victim cannot be quickly taken to a medical facility because of lack of transport or lack of a nearby facility, their chances of death are significantly increased. Likewise, anti-venoms may not be available throughout these areas either.

The saw-scaled viper is the deadliest snake on the planet. It doesn't have the most potent venom of all snakes, but it is irritable and aggressive and has frequent contact with people. Its venom is lethal, and it is found in Africa, southwestern Asia and India. They are also small and can hide easily. They may even be responsible for more human deaths than all other snake species combined.[18]

In some parts of the world, permanent disability is common from snakebites as well. This can be severe in the form of limb amputation in many cases. There are an estimated 400,000 permanent disabilities caused by snakebites every year worldwide.[12] Thankfully, we have good emergency access to care in the United States compared to most parts of the globe, so snakebite death and disability is rare.

In my personal experience, I have one major snake-related injury that I've treated. A patient tripped over an appliance when trying to run from a snake they identified in their house and fell and broke their wrist. The snake was a rat snake, which is nonvenomous. Sometimes the fear of something can lead us to injury rather than the thing itself, but it's often difficult to control your "fight or flight" response when you're reacting naturally.

Additionally, I have heard of one other interesting snake bite. A man was bitten by his pet king cobra and had to be monitored in an ICU and treated. The local hospital did not have the appropriate anti-venom since cobras are not native to the United States. The anti-venom had to be flown in by helicopter from a zoo in another state. The zoo kept the appropriate anti-venom on hand because they have a large exotic snake exhibit. Regardless, the man survived despite being bitten by a snake that is not endemic to the U.S., which goes to show that our emergency access is excellent for snakebites, although I'm sure the insurance company had a lot of questions regarding the circumstances of a cobra snakebite when they were covering the bill.

Why Insect Bites and Food Allergies Can Kill

Why do ant bites and bee stings have the potential to kill some people? While most people will only have a mild reaction to Hymenoptera venom, some people develop *anaphylaxis* or *anaphylactic shock* as a response to the venom. This same response develops in some individuals with various foods as well.

When I entered medical school, I thought the term *shock* only referred to a mental condition. The better term for this is *Acute Stress Reaction* and refers to mental stress as a result of a traumatic event. However, the term *shock* is much more commonly used by the medical community to refer to a circulatory system failure called *Circulatory Shock*. I was therefore confused when our physiology teacher in medical school first explained the concept to me, so I will try to educate you on what *shock* means in medical terms to medical providers. Keep in mind that there is no test for you at the end of this book so don't stress over the terms, just use it to enhance your understanding. If you're the type of person who doesn't care to know the details, feel free to skip to the section titled *Allergies* on page 204.

Shock or *Circulatory Shock* refers to a condition in which the body cannot meet the oxygen requirements of its various organs for a number of potential reasons.[19] This can be due to a dramatic increase in oxygen needs and the inability for the body to supply that amount, an inefficient use of oxygen, or a failure of the delivery systems themselves. You can ignore most of these definitions for the purposes of the book. We are going to discuss two major ones to help us understand how it can affect people.

Types of Shock

One type of shock called *Hemorrhagic Shock* happens when you lose too much blood. This is, perhaps, the easiest type of shock to understand conceptually. It's simple: if you lose too much blood, you cannot provide sufficient oxygen to the body. It's similar to your car running out of fuel. This happens after major blood losses, such as losing half of your total blood supply or more. This does not usually occur because of a small cut or bruise, but major blood loss after a severe trauma, such as internal bleeding from a car wreck or cutting an artery. Your body typically contains 5 L of blood in the circulatory system, which is approximately 1.32 gallons. Depending on the rate of the bleeding, hemorrhagic shock first starts as an increased heart rate as the body tries to increase the rate of blood circulation. If you have less blood but pump it quicker, then you can possibly keep up with the oxygen demand. As the blood loss worsens, the body will lose its ability to maintain the blood pressure. You need a certain amount of blood available to travel through the blood vessels, or else your heart cannot pump quickly enough to get oxygen to the places it needs to go.

We typically treat minor blood loss initially with intravenous fluid replacement. As you start to lose your ability to maintain appropriate blood pressure and your heart rate elevates, you require a blood transfusion. Fluids alone are not enough to fix the problem, and instead we must give you actual blood to both increase the amount of volume circulating in your body as well as provide the red blood cells capable of oxygen exchange. If major bleeding has occurred by the time you arrive to the hospital and you are in a state of hemorrhagic shock, transfusions are given ASAP.

Anaphylactic Shock is a different mechanism of circulatory collapse, but the end result is the same: the body cannot provide oxygen to its tissues, which can lead to organ failure and death. This is how people die from food and drug allergies or insect stings. The immune system is a wonderful part of our physiology, but when it malfunctions or runs haywire, it can lead to anaphylaxis, or anaphylactic shock. There are multiple types of antibodies in our immune system, and the one called *IgE* is responsible for many allergic reactions, including anaphylactic reactions. There are four major types of allergic reactions, and IgE is responsible for one of those types. It is involved in diseases such as allergic rhinitis (seasonal allergies) and asthma. With anaphylactic shock, however, the immune system takes it to the extreme.[20]

Anaphylaxis happens when your immune system overreacts to an environmental factor, such as a peanut or a bee sting. This is in lieu of a normal or mild response. In anaphylactic shock, the body releases multiple chemicals from the immune system in excessive amounts, which can affect the heart's ability to pump and the natural rhythm of the heart. These chemicals can also cause the body to lose control of its blood pressure regulation. All the blood vessels in the body can dilate at the same time.

Typically, your body directs blood traffic automatically through the *Autonomic Nervous System* depending on what your needs are at any given time. If you're trying to digest food after a meal, for example, the blood vessels constrict or narrow in the limbs and dilate in your digestive system so that your digestive system can use more oxygen to work more effectively. This is why you want to sit and nap after you eat a big meal, and going on a run sounds like a terrible idea (and it always sounds like a terrible idea to me anyway, to be honest). Alternatively, when you need to escape from a bear chasing you, your body needs more blood flow to the limb muscles so you can run faster. You don't need blood to go to the digestive system as much because it's not being used. It's a clever way of routing resources to the body parts being used at different times for different purposes.

If all your blood vessels dilated at the same time, however, that 5 liters of blood circulating cannot do its job of delivering oxygen effectively. The best analogy I can think of is when you're trying to take care of your children. You only have so much time and energy to spend in a single day. When one child is sick and you have to take off from work, you can survive. If you were in "anaphylactic shock" in your daily life, however, it would be ultimate chaos. Imagine all four of your children are sick with a stomach virus and you have it too. Then one of your parents gets ill and needs your help. And today, of all days, you are supposed to be delivering a speech for a project at work that you've been working on as the team leader for two years. If it goes well, you could get a great promotion, but your boss tells you that if you don't show up today, you'll be fired and you're the sole breadwinner for the family. Oh, and your dog just pooped all over your new bedspread you just bought that was very expensive and your husband just wrecked his car and he's in the hospital. You don't have the time and energy to deal with that on your own. Likewise, when all the blood vessels of the body are dilated, five liters of blood is not enough to deliver oxygen to everywhere.

With anaphylactic shock, the airway also swells in response to the hyperactive chemicals as well, which can cause the airway to spasm and essentially choke the victim. The quickest response to anaphylactic reactions is to administer *Epinephrine*, most commonly in the form of an EpiPen®. Epinephrine is the same thing as adrenaline, and it is a naturally occurring chemical in the body. EpiPens® contain a large quantity of epinephrine that can be directly injected into a muscle. Epinephrine will cause the blood vessels to constrict again, which returns the balance of the blood circulation and reduces the swelling in the airways. However, a single dose may not be enough. You should *ALWAYS* seek medical care if an anaphylactic reaction is suspected, even if the EpiPen® seems to be working.

Allergies

There are four types of allergic reactions the body can have to external triggers. The key is differentiating which reactions are anaphylactic, and which can potentially cause death. If your child ever has a reaction to something in the form of a rash or cough, the best thing to do is take a picture of the rash and take your child to the pediatrician. Urticaria, or hives, are raised lesions on the skin that can be a sign of a more severe allergic reaction, but they do not always indicate anaphylaxis.

In order to develop an allergy, usually someone has to least one prior exposure to the trigger, and sometimes further exposures can cause the reaction to worsen with time. In other words, just because your child doesn't react to an ant bite the first time they are bitten, they could develop severe reactions upon subsequent bites. Likewise, they may not react the first time they eat a peanut but could react in the future as their body builds an abnormal response to the trigger.

Our second son initially loved eating eggs, but he developed hives after eating them around age 8 months. From then on, we had to avoid feeding him eggs for a few months and then do a challenge at an allergist's office, which means we fed him eggs and watched him at the doctor's office for an extended period. He ended up not reacting to the eggs again and no longer has an allergic reaction to them, but he also lost his desire to eat eggs in the meantime, and he still doesn't like them at age 5.

So, what differentiates anaphylaxis from other reactions and what should you watch out for? The following are signs of anaphylactic allergic reactions[21]:

- Hives
- Puffiness of the face, eyelids, ears, mouth, hands, or feet
- Redness or itching of the skin
- Swelling or itching of the eyes
- Swelling of the tongue or throat

- Trouble breathing, wheezing, or a change in voice
- Vomiting or diarrhea
- Feeling dizzy or passing out

If you notice your child starting to develop a rash or reaction, monitor for the signs above. If they develop, you should call 911.

If your pediatrician deems appropriate, they will prescribe you an epinephrine auto-injector pen, brand name EpiPen®. You will need to learn how to use it and keep it with your child at all times. This means alerting the school and making sure they have one at their disposal. If you ever have to use the auto-injector pen, you should still call 911 because symptoms could return even if they resolve temporarily after the pen is used.

Lastly, I have included a list of the most common causes or triggers of anaphylaxis[22]:

- Peanuts, walnuts, and pecans
- Fish
- Shellfish
- Cow's Milk
- Eggs
- Latex (gloves or balloons commonly)
- Medications including ibuprofen and penicillin
- Insect stings, including bees, wasps, hornets, yellow jackets, and ants

If your child develops anaphylactic reactions, your pediatrician will likely refer you to a pediatric allergist. Your child may undergo allergy shots, which are shots of small doses of the trigger for your child. In small amounts, the triggering substance is less likely to cause a reaction. Over time, the dose of the allergy shot slowly increases, exposing to higher concentrations of the trigger. This sensitizes the body to the trigger, allowing it to be slowly exposed and hopefully reducing the chances that your child will overreact in a real-world exposure.

* * *

References

1. Conover M. Numbers of human fatalities, injuries, and illnesses in the United States due to wildlife. *Human-Wildlife Interactions*. Fall 2019 13(2):264-276.

2. Forrester JA, Weiser TG, Forrester JD. An Update on Fatalities Due to Venomous and Nonvenomous Animals in the United States (2008-2015). *Wilderness Environ Med*. Mar 2018;29(1):36-44. doi:10.1016/j.wem.2017.10.004

3. Shahbandeh M. Number of dogs in the United States from 2000 to 2017. Statista. Updated January 12, 2024. Accessed September 3, 2024. https://www.statista.com/statistics/198100/dogs-in-the-united-states-since-2000/

4. Number of people killed by animals each year in the US remains unchanged. Elsevier: ScienceDaily. Updated February 28, 2018. Accessed September 3, 2024. https://www.sciencedaily.com/releases/2018/02/180228112528.htm

5. The Schmidt sting pain index. Natural History Museum. Accessed September 3, 2024. https://www.nhm.ac.uk/discover/schmidt-pain-index-insect-stings.html

6. Initiation With Ants: National Geographic. National Geographic Channel YouTube Channel; December 21, 2007. https://www.youtube.com/watch?v=ZGIZ-zUvotM

7. LoVecchio F. Scorpion envenomation causing neuromuscular toxicity (United States, Mexico, Central America, and Southern Africa). UpToDate. Updated August 2024. Accessed September 3, 2024. https://www.uptodate.com/contents/scorpion-envenomation-causing-neuromuscular-toxicity-united-states-mexico-central-america-and-southern-africa

8. Swanson D, Vetter R, White J. Widow spider bites: Clinical manifestations and diagnosis. UpToDate. Updated August 2024. Accessed September 3, 2024. https://www.uptodate.com/contents/widow-spider-bites-clinical-manifestations-and-diagnosis

9. Vetter R, Swanson D. Bites of recluse spiders. UpToDate. Updated August 2024. Accessed September 3, 2024. https://www.uptodate.com/contents/bites-of-recluse-spiders

10. Genesis 3:15. The Holy Bible, New International Version https://www.bible.com/bible/111/GEN.3.15.niv

11. Snakes. Internet Center for Wildlife Damage Management. Accessed September 3, 2024. https://icwdm.org/species/reptiles/snakes/#:~:text=About%2015o%20species%20of%20snakes%20occur%20in,North%20America%2C%20of%20which%20over%2090%25%20are%20nonvenomous.

12. Pucca MB, Knudsen C, I SO, et al. Current Knowledge on Snake Dry Bites. *Toxins (Basel)*. Oct 22 2020;12(11)doi:10.3390/toxins12110668

13. Ruha M, spyres M. Evaluation and management of coral snakebites. UpToDate. Accessed September 3, 2024. https://www.uptodate.com/contents/evaluation-and-management-of-coral-snakebites?search=snake+bite&source=search_result&selectedTitle=4%7E44&usage_type=default&display_rank=4

14. White J. Snakebites worldwide: Management. UpToDate. Updated July 15, 2024. Accessed September 3, 2024. https://www.uptodate.com/contents/snakebites-worldwide-management?search=snake%20bite&source=search_result&selectedTitle=1%7E53&usage_type=default&display_rank=1

15. What to Do to Protect Yourself From Animals After a Disaster. Center for Disease Control: Natural Disasters and Severe Weather. Updated February 8, 2024. Accessed September 3, 2024. https://www.cdc.gov/natural-disasters/response/what-to-do-protect-yourself-from-animals-after-a-disaster.html?CDC_AAref_Val= https://www.cdc.gov/disasters/snakebite.html

16. Elflein J. Deadliest animals worldwide by annual number of human deaths as of 2022. Statista. Updated May 22, 2024. Accessed September 3, 2024. https://www.statista.com/statistics/448169/deadliest-creatures-in-the-world-by-number-of-human-deaths/

17. Snakebite envenoming. World Health Organization. Updated September 12, 2023. Accessed September 3, 2024. https://www.who.int/news-room/fact-sheets/detail/snakebite-envenoming#:~:text=Key%20facts.%20An%20estimated%205.4%20million%20people%20worldwide%20are#:~:text=Key%20facts.%20An%20estimated%205.4%20million%20people%20worldwide%20are

18. Wallach V. Saw-scaled Viper. Britannica. Accessed September 3, 2024. https://www.britannica.com/animal/saw-scaled-viper

19. Gaieski D, Mikkelsen M. Definition, classification, etiology, and pathophysiology of shock in adults. UpToDate. Updated June 16, 2023. Accessed September 3, 2024. https://www.uptodate.com/contents/definition-classification-etiology-and-pathophysiology-of-shock-in-adults#H532957492

20. Kemp S. Pathophysiology of anaphylaxis. UpToDate. Updated March 6, 2024. Accessed September 3, 2024. https://www.uptodate.com/contents/pathophysiology-of-anaphylaxis?topicRef=1594&source=related_link

21. Patient education: Anaphylaxis (The Basics). UpToDate. Accessed September 3, 2024. https://www.uptodate.com/contents/anaphylaxis-the-basics?topicRef=106778&source=see_link

22. Anaphylaxis. The American College of Allergy, Asthma & Immunology. Updated January 29, 2018. Accessed September 3, 2024. https://acaai.org/allergies/symptoms/anaphylaxis/

Chapter 19

Deaths in the Developing World

What about children outside of the United States? We live in a wonderful time in history, and presumably medical care is only going to get better. However, many parts of the world have very limited access to the latest and greatest medical technologies, and even some parts have very limited access to basic hygiene, such as a toilet. In my opinion, it is worth taking the time to review all-cause worldwide mortality in children ages 5-14 to highlight some of the differences between the United States and the developing world. I will break this section down in a bird's eye view. The data in this chapter is pulled from *Our World in Data*, an epidemiology and statistical resource that aggregates multiple data sources.

In the year 2019, the worldwide causes of death in children ages 5-14 were as follows[1]:

1. Road accidents at 55,268
2. Cancers at 54,877
3. Diarrheal diseases at 52,552

Bare Bones

4. Lower respiratory infections (pneumonia, for example) at 42,387
5. Malaria at 39,550
6. Drowning at 36,657
7. HIV/AIDS at 27,492
8. Digestive diseases at 19,844
9. Cardiovascular disease at 17,949
10. Tuberculosis at 15,444

Other "dishonorable" mentions include nutritional deficiencies at 8,611 and protein-energy malnutrition at 6,948. Notice the differences and similarities to the worldwide view and the United States. The worldwide view does contain all "first world" or developed countries as well as all of the "third world" or developing countries. I will point out that certain countries in the developing world are probably less accurate at tracking this data effectively due to lack of resources and large rural populations, so the numbers for some of these fatalities may be more severe than actually recorded. If you look at just the "Low Income" category of *Our World in Data*, the top three causes are diarrheal disease, malaria, and HIV/AIDS in this age group.

For children under 5, the leading causes of death were as follows[2]:

1. Low birth weight at 1.7 million
2. Child wasting (starvation) at 874,543
3. Household air pollution at 457,920
4. Unsafe water source 419,920
5. Poor sanitation at 279,618
6. No access to handwashing facility at 255,025
7. Outdoor particulate matter pollution at 233,454
8. Child stunting/malnutrition at 164,237
9. Non-exclusive breastfeeding at 139,732
10. Secondhand smoke at 46,580

Just take a moment to review these two lists. The good news is that these numbers have decreased significantly over the past 10 to 15 years, which means progress is certainly being made. These charts are reminiscent of past times in the U.S. when the life expectancy was lower because many children would die before they reached the age of one. If you compare our list in the U.S. to the worldwide list, you notice that birth problems and true medical disorders are the causes of most deaths in American children, whereas worldwide, the causes seem a lot more preventable. Though my purpose of the book is to highlight what makes me nervous as a physician who specializes in injury, we need to recognize that other parents in other parts of the world love their children just as much as we love ours, and they would do anything to protect them and keep them safe. Those parents want the same things for their children as we want for ours: health, success, and happiness. I would hate to think of my child dying because they did not have access to a bathroom or soap or nutrition.

Malaria and tuberculosis are still major causes of death in parts of the world, and HIV/AIDS is also a common source of death. This is a very sad reality for many parents and children. They are at risk of death from issues that we have proven are preventable and treatable by our own success in the U.S. Certainly, malaria and tuberculosis have a geographic component, but the point still remains.

Pedialyte® is an oral rehydration liquid that is specifically aimed at dehydration in children and infants, particularly with diarrheal illness. Although I cannot find a specific source on this, I have heard it suggested multiple times that Pedialyte and similar oral rehydration therapies save more children's lives worldwide per year than most other medications, probably including antibiotics. It's amazing that something can be so powerful but also so cheap. Increasing its availability in poorer nations makes a huge difference.

I will make a plug here for *Mission: Hope*. This is a Christian faith-based organization that goes out to multiple areas of the world and provides relief in areas that are extremely poor. I had the fortune to do multiple trips with them many years ago to the Dominican Republic (DR). While there, we met with a local pastor who took us to slums filled with Haitian refugees. The Dominican Republic and Haiti share an island called Hispaniola, but the Haitian side is much poorer. Even before the devastating earthquake in 2012 and more recently in 2021, many refugees lived in the DR and were confined to slums called *bates* (bah-teys). Since then, the problems have only worsened. Imagine mud huts in tightly confined spaces with public water sources from nearby water trenches. Often, these are the source of both drinking water and a toilet, whether directly or indirectly by runoff from rainwater. In the *bates*, we volunteered resources to build latrines, which were essentially toilets. They consisted of a large deep hole covered by a concrete slab with a small hole in the center. We then built a solid wooden structure around the concrete slab for privacy. Think of it like a permanent porta potty. These cost approximately $450 to build at the time, and they made a huge impact on those communities. It allowed families to break the cycle of contamination in the water source. A lot of the families valued the security of their latrines more than their own houses and placed padlocks on their latrines because of the value of privacy and sanitation.

It sounds odd to a lot of us who have never had to live like that, but it is incredible to think about the value a toilet can bring to a household and a community. It can mean the difference in life and death in communities when it comes to diarrheal illness. Fortunately for us in the developed world, we do not have these kinds of worries for the most part. We know there is medical care and infrastructure in place to prevent a lot of these deaths compared to the developing world. If you are looking for causes to donate to with either time or finances, look into these types of projects. They provide great benefits at relatively low costs and can save the lives of children. These families love their children just as much we love ours, and there is still much work to be done.

If you are of a mindset to do some good for your fellow man, there are many excellent organizations that work to bring healthy water, nutrition, and better hygiene to third world countries. You can research a reputable non-profit organization to help contribute. *World Vision* and *Samaritan's Purse* are two good ones in addition to *Mission: Hope*. There are many good ones out there. Just make sure you do your research and pay attention to how much of your dollar actually goes toward the goal rather than overhead cost of the organization.

* * *

References

1. Causes of death in children aged 5 to 14, World, 2019. Our World in Data. Accessed September 25, 2024. https://ourworldindata.org/grapher/causes-of-death-in-5-14-year-olds?time=2019

2. Deaths by risk factor for under-5s, World, 2021. Our World in Data. Accessed September 3, 2024. https://ourworldindata.org/grapher/deaths-by-risk-under5s

Chapter 20

Summary

Throughout the book, we've gone in depth with some checklists for certain scenarios, and I promised to try to simplify rather than overly complicate. So, what's really important? We've talked about topics separately, but let's take a more general view.

Break it up into two ways to reduce the chances of something truly awful happening to your child. Childproof (and periodically re-check) so you can prevent catastrophe, and constantly monitor during high-risk activities. This book and its recommendations can be summarized in these two points alone. Hopefully, the childproofing recommendations from the prior chapters follow a commonsense pattern, and I have helped add something to your household safety. More importantly, I hope I identified high risk activities for you, and that you will draw more attention to the parts of your day that truly matter for your child's safety.

If you can't remember a laundry list, then make it simple. Childproof by securing dangerous places and by not putting yourself into bad positions. Set yourself up for success. If you lock dangers away, such as firearms, household cleaners, and medicines, then it's not going to be a risk that you have to worry about. Like I have stated in a previous chapter, you cannot control how other people drive, but you can ensure your child is properly restrained and make sure you keep up with appropriate maintenance for your car. There are certain high-risk activities during which you must at least have a moderate amount of caution (playgrounds) and others when you have to be on high alert at all times (swimming pools). If you are planning on going to an event including a swimming pool when you are by yourself with three children, it's probably best not to go if you cannot get another adult to help. If you go with another adult, make sure you have defined roles for which children you are each going to be responsible for around the pool.

Children are absolutely going to find ways to accidentally hurt themselves. I swear our children make it a 24/7 job for themselves. You cannot stop it completely. Life is full of risk, but life is good. It's how they learn and grow. Focus on preventing the risks that will hurt them most and try to enjoy the rest. Focus on what really matters, and just use common sense. As the orthopedists' go-to textbook for childhood fractures *Rockwood and Wilkin's Fractures in Children* so wisely states, "Play is an essential element of a child's life. It enhances physical development and fosters social interaction.[1]" You cannot stop children from being children, but you can do your best to put your effort where it matters most.

Part of our job as parents and caretakers is to help our kids understand the consequences of the risks they take. With clear safety rules and clear consequences for breaking them, we can aid in this understanding. While we may suffer some backlash and tantrums in the moment, missing out on an activity or toy due to danger and maintaining consistency in following through will result in a more aware child and hopefully fewer accidents. For instance, when a child jumps into the pool before you are ready for them to, make them sit out for a prolonged period of time. Have a "no exceptions" policy with these type of safety events. It's one thing if your child says a foul word (which they clearly learned from their mother!) or hits their brother. It's another thing if your children are pulling each other down in the pool. Do not let these episodes slip. Repeat the safety rules every time you go somewhere new and even sometimes at familiar places.

The older your child gets, the more you will learn about them and their ability to handle certain situations. You cannot keep them in a bubble forever, but you also will learn your child's ability to handle different circumstances. For instance, some children may be more responsible when it comes to riding a scooter or driving a golf cart as they get into their teenage years while others may be a danger to themselves and others. Know the situation, and know your child.

Often you might leave your children in the care of others, such as your family or with a sitter. While you may remember some of these important tips, grandparents have not had to be responsible for children for a long time period, and they might have forgotten some of the finer details of appropriate child monitoring. Likewise, some of the rules may have changed with respect to car seats and boosters since you were a child. Provide them with some reminders, especially about pools and bathtubs. You can do it politely, but if you hit the high points, it may serve you well.

One final caution: don't let social pressure affect your judgment. If you've been a parent for a long time, you know that everyone tends to do things differently. Some parents are more cautious about certain dangers, and others are more relaxed. If you are moving to a new area and someone invites you to their pool, but it's going to just be you with three children, it's better to say no if you have multiple non-swimmers to worry about. Likewise, if other parents choose not to make their children wear helmets, stick to your guns with your own children. Don't let your children or other parents pressure you into bending or breaking rules or making you uncomfortable with safety. All it takes is one quick mistake, and it could mean severe injury or death for a child that otherwise might have been preventable.

I hope you have enjoyed this book and will refer to it at times for reference. Share it with a friend and use the information in this book to augment your parenting and make it a more enjoyable experience so you can appropriately direct your stress and learn to let stress out during the other times. Enjoy parenting! They do tend to grow up quickly, so keep the main things the main things. Let them live a little, but also keep your eye on the parts of your days that are higher risk. Sticks and stones may break your bones, but keep it reasonable! And if all else fails, there are always medical providers nearby to help.

* * *

References

1. David Skaggs MD, John Flynn MD, Peter Waters MD. *Rockwood and Wilkins' Fractures in Children*. 8th ed. Wolters Kluwer Health; 2015:1288.

Chapter 21

Injury Appendix: What To Do

Since I'm an orthopedic surgeon, I'd be remiss to not include a segment for dealing with children's injuries for worried parents. Remember, 42% of boys and 27% of girls will sustain a broken bone prior to the age of 16.[1] In this chapter, I will explain how to approach an injury to a limb if you are concerned about a broken bone among other topics.

Topics covered include:

- Broken bones
- Joint dislocations
- Nursemaid's elbow
- Head injuries
- Lacerations and stitches
- Lip and tongue bites
- Tooth knocked out
- Common animal bites
- Chemical contact and burns
- Ingestion

For the purposes of this chapter, I will refer to both the Emergency Room (ER) and Emergency Department (ED) interchangeably.

Disclaimer: I am not your medical provider, and I have not evaluated you or your child for any medical problems, so I cannot provide specific advice for specific injury episodes. This chapter is intended to provide helpful tips on what to watch out for and when to seek further treatment. If you have ANY concerns, take your child to a medical provider for an evaluation. Do not use this book or chapter to make medical decisions on your own.

Broken Bones

Step 1: Don't Panic

Most falls do not result in a fracture. As a reminder, a fracture and a break are the same thing to an orthopedist. If your child is less than the age of 18-24 months, it is unlikely your child has broken a bone unless a severe fall happens, which usually is a result of the child being placed too high on a bed or piece of furniture and falling off, or even down a set of stairs.

The most common sign that a fracture has occurred in a younger child is refusal to use the limb in question. If they will let you move the arm without fussing, it's unlikely to be broken. The same goes for legs. If the child refuses to walk, it is more concerning for a fracture. Also, children are usually more distressed and more difficult to calm after breaking a bone than they normally are from a similar fall.

Take a deep breath and don't panic. Fractures hurt but they are not usually the type of emergency that will cause long lasting harm if they are not treated immediately. In other words, you don't have to rush; it's not a heart attack. Of course, there are always exceptions such as open fractures or loss of pulse, and I will define these below, but in general, pain is the biggest problem, and pain won't kill your child. Even if the limb loses blood flow from a blood vessel injury, you usually have time to fix the issue if treated promptly, within 6 to 8 hours.

Step 2: Give it Time

This is more for a fracture that does not cause gross deformity to the limb. "Gross deformity" is a nice way of saying that the limb "don't look right." If the limb looks swollen, it may be a sign of fracture, but it could also just be a bruise. Bones contain a lot of blood cells within their internal structure. So mild to severe swelling can accompany fractures, but it can also be present from sprains or normal bruises. If the limb clearly has gross deformity, you will notice. The arm will be crooked or maybe the ankle will be sticking out at a funny angle. If there is gross deformity, it is not appropriate to do a period of observation and you should take your child promptly to an emergency department.

If the limb has only mild swelling or otherwise looks okay, do a period of observation. If your child settles down and starts using the limb again, it is probably fine. If they start limping after an injury, it may be a sign of a fracture, but in the absence of swelling or deformity, it is likely okay to wait until the next day to see a provider. The same thing goes for refusal to use an arm. My recommendation is to give the child a dose of ibuprofen (Advil®, Motrin® brand names) and/or acetaminophen (Tylenol®) shortly after the injury. The dosages vary based on the weight and age of the child. They can be safely taken together, and ibuprofen is generally the better pain reliever. Be cautious about which medications you give because some medications are not approved for children under certain ages.

Older children can communicate with you, so it is easier to diagnose the problem. They can tell you if it's their ankle or their knee that hurts. Likewise, they can indicate how severe the pain is and can help decide if they need to be seen urgently or if it could wait a day.

Step 3: Call or Visit a Provider

If you're concerned about a true emergency, the ER is your best bet. Urgent care facilities are excellent options as well, especially for injuries that do not include severe deformity. They generally cost less, have shorter waiting times, and can get you the same result as the ER with initial treatment. The ER is better for the obviously deformed injuries in case a *reduction* needs to be performed, although urgent care facilities can generally make this decision as well and get you quickly to an ER if needed. *Reduction* is the term for setting the bone straight and often requires some sort of anesthesia that can be performed in the either the ED or the operating room. Either an emergency medicine physician or an orthopedist will typically perform the reduction.

Also, feel free to call your pediatrician or a local orthopedic office to see if there's availability. Even if the pediatrician's office does not have X-ray capabilities, they may have a connection to an orthopedist's office and be able to get you in more quickly than if you called the office directly.

Often, if you visit an ER or an urgent care, your child will be placed into a splint or a cast and sent to see an orthopedist on a weekday during normal business hours. Don't be mad or surprised if they cannot get you in immediately to an orthopedist. Most injuries are treatable with casting or bracing alone, but a non-orthopedic provider may not know the best treatment for the injury, so don't be surprised if the orthopedist tells you something different than the ER provider.

If you have a pediatric ER or hospital near your place of injury, it may be a better idea to take your child to that facility over another one. Pediatric ERs and hospitals specialize in children's injuries and will likely be more equipped to handle the needs of a child over other institutions.

Exceptions due to true emergencies:

What should you be looking out for that would cause more concern and prompt an immediate visit to the ER? I'll try to mention the important ones.

The most common true emergency would be obvious deformity or even a floppy limb. If you see pressure on the skin or the limb clearly doesn't look right, go to an emergency facility. Though not usually limb threatening, the best way to get the pain to improve and prevent injury from continued awkward pressure on the nerves and blood vessels is to have the bones set. Too much pressure on the skin from the bone pressing on it underneath can eventually cause the overlying skin to die, which is a big deal. Fortunately, this is relatively uncommon in children.

Pulseless limbs are an absolute emergency. If you know how to check a pulse, check a pulse. This is almost always accompanied by severe deformity or rapid swelling because the artery gets injured. The artery is the main blood source to the limb, and sometimes there is more than one artery depending on the limb and the location within the limb. Arterial injury can occur from simple pressure pinching the artery off or from the sharp end of a bone cutting the artery. This type of injury is rare and is not usually caused by a ground level fall but something more severe, such as a bicycle crash or high contact sports injury. I have also seen it in high falls from swing sets directly onto the elbow, and it's almost always obvious that it's a severe injury. If you do not know how to check for a pulse, the other sign to look for is loss of color in the hand or foot. If the hand or foot becomes cool or pale, it may not necessarily mean the vessel is injured, but it is at least enough to indicate that an emergent evaluation by a medical provider is necessary.

The other exception to watch for is severe bleeding accompanied by deformity. I am not referring to a small cut or a scrape on the skin but rather a deep bleed. This could range from a hole in the skin the size of pen tip to a large laceration. Sometimes this can indicate that there is an *open fracture* which means the bone has been exposed to the outside world through the skin. The bone may have poked through the skin from the inside out, or maybe an object cut down into the skin from the outside in. In severe cases, this will scare the heck out of you, but it will at least be obvious. You won't be checking this book as a reference in such an event. Sometimes the bleeding can be subtle, but if it happens, it needs urgent treatment. Bone that has been through the skin is at risk for bacterial infection. Bacterial infection in bone can impair its healing ability as well as require substantial durations of antibiotic treatments (6 weeks or more) and even surgery to heal. The best way to prevent an infection in the fracture is quick administration of an antibiotic by a medical professional, ideally within an hour. Do not take a supply from some you have leftover at home.

All-in-all, the truly emergent situations should be fairly obvious and probably instinctual. The best thing you can do regardless of the situation is to not panic. Most of the time when a child breaks a bone, however, the most traumatic part of it is the pain, and the bone will heal as long as it is treated appropriately.

Dislocations and Joint Injuries

Joint dislocations are when two or more bones that connect to one another become disconnected. There are different types of joints, but they typically all have tissues that surround the bone ends and keep them tightly in contact with one another. Shoulders are the most commonly dislocated joint. Other common dislocations include fingers, elbows, and patellae (kneecaps).

If you suspect a dislocation has happened, you should seek medical attention urgently. It's usually pretty obvious and painful because the limb in question will look crooked. If joints stay dislocated for too long (usually more than a few hours), the bone ends can start pressing on blood vessels or nerves and damage them. In some cases, it can also kill the skin overlying the joint, which is a potentially disastrous situation. Most joint dislocations require some kind of sedation with medications, so I recommend visiting an ER, but you can usually travel in your own vehicle without calling emergency Medical Services (EMS/911). If the ER physician cannot reduce, or put the joint back into place, the injury, an orthopedist may be called to help.

You will then be directed to follow up with an orthopedist. One situation that frustrates parents/patients in my practice is the assumption that an MRI is needed or already scheduled the first time they visit my office after an injury. MRI stands for Magnetic Resonance Imaging and shows the soft tissue structures such as ligaments and tendons that normal X-rays do not. MRIs take a long time (20 or more minutes) and require careful scheduling. It is rare to be able to get an MRI within the next day or two. Depending on the facility, urgent MRIs can be performed within a business week. Likewise, just because a non-orthopedic provider suggests you need an MRI does not necessarily mean that it's true. Trust the orthopedic provider to direct you appropriately. MRIs might be ordered on some joint dislocations depending on the situation, but it is not necessarily routine.

Nursemaid's Elbow

This is more of a specific one, but this is a somewhat common injury in smaller children, generally occurring between ages 1 to 4.[2] There are two bones in the forearm, the radius and the ulna. The part of the radius that is within the elbow joint is flat so that the radius can spin around the ulna, which allows our forearm to rotate for tasks such as twisting doorknobs. In younger children, the supporting ligaments around this part of the joint are relatively weak and this part of the radius can either partially or fully dislocate from the joint. This can be difficult to see on an x-ray. The child usually becomes very fussy and refuses to use the arm and will hold it close to their body. If you try to move their elbow, they become very agitated or upset.

Nursemaid's elbow dislocations occur usually from the child hyperextending their elbow or from an adult picking the child up by their forearm. The classic culprit is from a parent swinging their child back and forth for fun while picking the child up by their hands or forearms, which pulls through the elbow and dislodges the radius.

There are two simple maneuvers that allow us to "reduce" or put the radius back into its socket. Once or twice in my career, I have had children around age 2 with no apparent x-ray findings in my office. I perform the maneuver and within 5 minutes the child will use their arm normally and stop fussing.

One of my sons has suffered from a nursemaid's elbow multiple times, maybe four in total from what I can remember. The first time occurred after he flipped off a rocking chair and did a handspring and hyperextended his elbow. I performed the maneuver, felt it click back in, and he was happy within minutes. After that, however, it became easier for it to dislocate. If this ever happens to your child once, it might happen multiple times until they "outgrow" the problem.

Head Injuries

Probably the most concerning injury for parents is a head injury as they have the potential to be serious. I have already discussed in prior chapters about the risks of head injury and the ways they happen. For this section, I am mainly discussing young children outside of sports. There is a large difference between a minor trauma with a minor injury and a major trauma with a major injury. There can also be major traumas with minor injuries and vice versa. This section is dedicated to explaining the signs of a potentially bad head injury. When in doubt, you should *always* take your child to the ED or even call 911. I will outline the biggest warning signs so you can know what to watch out for and be alert. Remember, I am a physician, but I am not *your* physician. I am giving general information, and I am in no way able to direct you through all possibilities because there are always exceptions.

Bare Bones

Step 1: Don't Panic

Again, don't panic. Try to keep calm and assess the situation before reacting. Crying is a completely normal and appropriate response. It is normal for children to be upset and cry when they are injured (and sometimes even the parent!).

Step 2: Watch for Warning Signs

The biggest warning signs are as follows[3]:

- Pits or indentations in your child's skull
- Failure to respond to voice or lightly touching the child or lethargy
- Loss of consciousness, even briefly
- Seizures, which show as repetitive rapid muscle movements or even rigid locking of the child's body
- Confusion or amnesia
- Abnormal behavior
- Large swelling in the scalp (otherwise known as a hematoma), particularly in children under the age of 6 months
- Vomiting
- Swelling and/or bruising around the eye sockets (known as "racoon eyes" for its appearance)
- Swelling and/or bruising around the areas behind the ears
- Clear fluid leaking from the ears or nose (potentially may be cerebrospinal fluid)
- Child's pupils being two different sizes

Remember that the vast majority of head injuries do not result in permanent damage. Pay attention to the mechanism of injury, i.e., how it happened. A fall from ground height for a two-year-old on average is around 33 inches (because that's how tall the average two-year-old is), and that is way different than a fall from a two-story window. If you notice *any* of the above signs, seek emergency care promptly. Remember, crying is a *normal* response. Young children should cry after a hit to the head. They should *not* be lethargic or vomit or have any of the other signs previously mentioned. True lethargy is when the child is not responding to questions well and appears drowsy. Lethargy is not an appropriate reaction after a fall or injury and is a sign of a worse injury that should be evaluated by a medical professional. *Any* loss of consciousness, even briefly, is *not* a normal response and can be a sign of a potential surgical emergency, so promptly get the child to the ER.

Step 3: If ever in doubt, seek help

I think most parents would use their common sense in this type of situation. If something just doesn't seem right, seek help. Earlier in the book, I recounted the tale of my son falling down a set of stairs. He was crying appropriately, had a small, flat bruise on the side of his head, but he was moving all his limbs. I still panicked and we rushed off to the ER. He thankfully only had a mild concussion and nothing severe. I was barely into my second year of residency at the time and knew a lot less than I do now. But seeing him go through that was a big lesson for me. Kids are incredibly resilient, but I am still glad that I had him evaluated. Do not hesitate to seek an emergency evaluation if there's any doubt at all. Sure, you might get an ER bill, but it is sometimes worth the security of knowing and not missing anything. If you are on the fence about observing your child for a period of time before calling a physician, make sure you have ruled out the above warning signs for potentially significant head injury.

The reality is that most head injuries are not serious and at worst cause concussions without long-lasting effects. Leave it up to emergency physicians, however, if you are worried. They may simply observe the child for a few hours. One of the most common ways to evaluate more severe head injuries is through a computed tomography (CT) scan, which is a type of imaging that can be performed on the brain. We generally try to avoid CT scans in children because they emit a large amount of radiation, so there are specific criteria used by those physicians to determine if a CT scan is likely needed or not, and CT scans are uncommonly used in minor head injury.

Lacerations and Stitches

Laceration is a medical term for a cut. There are multiple layers of skin, and the depth of the laceration is what determines whether a stitch is needed or not. In general, if the cut is not very deep and you feel like you can still see a layer of skin at the base of the laceration, it probably does not need a stitch. However, if you cannot see the base, or there is a large gap, it is likely that a stitch would be beneficial.

The main reason we suture (another term for sew or stitch) wounds is for a quicker recovery with better cosmetic appearance. A lot of wounds that we suture will in fact heal fine on their own if given time but will leave a bigger and uglier scar. However, larger lacerations (think wide open gashes that are multiple inches long) become an issue with infection prevention, and the stitch does more than just improve the healing time and the final appearance of the scar.

There are three ways to close a laceration, one is with a classic suture material, the second is with skin staples, and the third is with a surgical skin glue (most common brand is *Dermabond*™). Typically, the suture method requires an initial injection into the surrounding area with a numbing medicine to allow for appropriate cleaning to be performed followed by suture placement. If non-dissolvable sutures are used, then the sutures must be removed at a later time, five to fourteen days depending on the body area (shorter for face, longer for a limb). The advantage of surgical skin glue is that numbing medicine is typically not required, although the glue itself can certainly sting for a minute. The compound is very similar to super glue and typically dries within 30 to 60 seconds. It also creates a watertight seal and will peel off on its own with time, so removal is not necessary with another trip to the physician's office. Skin glue by itself does not work as well for larger lacerations or certain parts of the body with a lot of movement, such as the skin over the knee..

So what do you do if you think your child needs stitches?

Step 1: Hold pressure!

Most bleeding can easily be stopped by simply holding pressure on the wound. It is amazing how even medical providers can forget this at times. It may take a couple of minutes to stop, but the best way to get the blood to clot is to hold solid, consistent pressure for a few minutes continuously. Do not take pressure off to view the wound or the clot may be disrupted. First, get the majority of the bleeding to stop by holding pressure. Then you can take a closer look at and clean the wound. Dying from "bleeding out" is very rare from any sort of trauma from a ground level fall or a limb laceration. Holding appropriate pressure will often do the trick, even in severe bleeds. Some severe situations may require up to 15 minutes of pressure. You may also use ice packs to hold pressure if available.

By the way, scalps bleed. They bleed a lot. The scalp has a lot of blood vessels, and small lacerations can look like a life-threatening hemorrhage if you're not used to seeing blood. The same rule applies: hold pressure.

When I was in kindergarten, I fell from the monkey bars at the school playground. I have a vivid memory of having sharp pain but not much else. I was in a rush because the whistle to come inside blew, and I was racing back to get my spot in line: I put my hand on my head, and I remember the paraprofessional's face of terror as I pulled my hand away. My entire hand was covered in blood and then I started to feel a drip down my head onto my nose. In retrospect, a child's hand is not big compared to an adult, but it seemed like a lot of blood at the time. My mother was called and brought a change of clothes because she was told I'd had "an accident." She thought I had wet myself. My father is a general surgeon, and she took me to his office. He sutured my head up, and I still have a scar to this day. But I survived without long lasting effects, though my wife probably swears I've had a brain injury at some point growing up.

Step 2: Clean the wound

The most important step to do is to clean the laceration to prevent infection. Infected wounds, particularly before the days of antibiotics, could cause loss of limb or even death by overwhelming infection in the bloodstream, called *sepsis*, though this was not usually true of smaller wounds. If you clean a laceration well enough, antibiotics are not often necessary. We typically reserve antibiotics for an open fracture site or deep punctures into the skin or vital organs or extremely large lacerations that require surgical treatment to appropriately cleanse the wound safely. Antibiotics are often necessary after certain animal bites as well. A tetanus shot or booster shot may be necessary depending on the last time your child had one.

What is tetanus and why do we need a shot for it? Tetanus is a condition caused by bacteria named *Clostridium tetani*. These bacteria are commonly present in ground materials, such as grass or soil. If infection sets in, it causes severe spasms and can lead to death. It is preventable by the tetanus vaccine, which is given as part of the routine vaccination series if your child is on schedule.

The best way to cleanse a laceration is with running water. As we say in surgery, "the solution to pollution is dilution." Run a bunch of water over the wound to essentially dilute the area out. Subsequently, you can clean with either hydrogen peroxide or an alcohol wipe. Betadine is an iodine-based cleaning solution that may be present in some first aid kits and also works well. Betadine can stain clothing, so be careful with it around clothes you want to keep intact. Alcohol stings, which children (and adults, for that matter!) hate. Betadine and hydrogen peroxide typically do not. Sometimes cleansing the wound may stir up the bleeding, but just hold pressure again with a clean wet cloth or gauze.

Step 3 (optional): Visit a provider

This is a tricky part to give advice on because many times it requires an actual look at the wound before I can tell someone if stitches are necessary. I get texts from time to time from our friends asking if a wound needs stitches. Usually, I can tell from a phone picture. Your best bet is to know a medical provider well enough to contact them for a quick picture (how did we ever survive before smart phones?). In the case that you do not know anyone well enough, try to stick to what I told you above. If you cannot see the base of the wound, go see someone. If it seems like there is some skin-like tissue underneath that is just a lighter color than the skin and the laceration is fairly small, you may be okay to observe it. Sometimes the wound may keep reopening every time you get it to stop bleeding and you find yourself having to hold more pressure. It is best to go see a provider in this situation. They may just end up putting a Band-Aid on it, but at least you will sleep easy.

Urgent cares are your best bet most of the time in this scenario. Some urgent cares even have online check-ins now, so you don't have to sit in the waiting room for very long. Even if you have to wait, the wait time is likely to be less than your local ER and often the bill is much smaller. These centers are perfectly capable of handling treatment of these wounds with a few exceptions, which include eyelids, eyebrows, or anything crossing the lip border. These areas can be a bit more tedious to repair, and while a scar is inevitable, you want the best cosmetic outcome. This may require an Ear, Nose, and Throat (ENT) surgeon, plastic surgeon, or general surgeon.

Lip and Tongue Bites

Step 1: Hold Pressure

Oral tissues generally heal very well and very quickly because they have excellent blood supply. However, they also bleed a lot because of the robust blood supply. It may be alarming when you see it, but hold pressure and the bleeding will stop.

Step 2: When to see a provider

The most current recommendations to repair a tongue laceration suggest that the laceration does *not* need repair if it does not gape or if it is less than two centimeters (approximately 1 inch) as long as the tissues come together when the tongue is at rest in the mouth.[4] This includes lacerations that go all the way through the tongue, particularly in younger children. Lacerations that might need to be repaired include lacerations that are causing the tongue to flap apart because it goes out through the side of the tongue or front of the tongue, like a snake tongue. When in doubt, call a medical provider.

Lip lacerations are a little trickier. If they are on the outside of the lip, the safest thing to do is have a provider look at it. The truth is that the lip will likely heal on its own without infection, but scarring can be the issue and cause cosmetic deformity, particularly on the upper lip. Thus, an ED physician or surgeon may need to suture the wound to ensure that scarring is minimal. If the child bites inside of the lip or mouth, these rarely need medical treatment. These tissues are designed to heal easily from self-inflicted bites because they occur so frequently.

What if a Tooth Gets Knocked Out?

Step 1: Shove it back in

If a child's permanent tooth is knocked out, there is a decently high chance that it will survive if replanted quickly. Do not wait for a provider. Do your best to place the tooth back in its place. Handle the tooth by the crown and not the root. Try to match its original orientation. If there is debris on the tooth, rinse it with milk. If you do not have milk quickly available, use the child's saliva. Do not scrub the tooth or try to clean it. Only remove large debris with a quick rinse. If the socket is bleeding, you may need to quickly wash the area to remove larger clots that are keeping the tooth from settling back into its place. Then, have the child bite or use their hand to hold the tooth in place.[5]

Tooth survival is time dependent. Some studies have suggested 85-97% survival if replanted within 5 minutes with as low as zero percent if you wait an hour, so do this quickly.

Step 2: Call a dentist or other dental professional (oral surgeon)

If you cannot call an office directly, go to the nearest ED. Urgent cares are unlikely to help in this situation because often dental providers do not have privileges to provide care at these facilities.

If you cannot replant the tooth for some reason, then store the tooth appropriately. The best option is to place it into cold milk and then pack the milk in a bag of ice. This preserves the viability of the cells at the root of the tooth. The second-best solution available to you is the child's saliva. As gross as it may be, have them spit into a container and place the tooth into it.

Common Animal Bites

Step 1: Cleanse the wound

As with other lacerations, control the bleeding by holding pressure and then cleanse the wound with low pressure water followed by alcohol, peroxide, or betadine. Cover the wound(s) with a bandage.

Step 2: Call or visit a provider

For deep penetrating bites, it's best to let a physician help you make decisions about further treatment. This excludes bites that do not penetrate the skin. Cat bites, for instance, may seem harmless, but they can cause some of the worst problems because their teeth are sharp and needle-like. They are more likely to bury bacteria deep below the skin, and since their teeth do not usually crush or tear, they may not leave a bad laceration. However, this also traps the bacteria in without allowing an exit path through the wound. In the hands and fingers, this can cause infection in the tendon sheaths, which can cause disability if left untreated. On elbows or forearms, infection can occur deep in the bone or the joint if the tooth penetrates that far. Antibiotics may be necessary for prevention depending on the severity of the bite. You might be less likely to think it necessary to take a child in for a cat bite because it doesn't leave big lacerations like a dog bite, but cat bites are more often associated with infections.

Dog bites are more likely to crush or tear tissues. They typically leave bigger holes in the skin or tissue, which allows easier outlets for bacteria and better areas to irrigate with water. However, dog bites can cause more serious injury to the blood vessels or nerves. Depending on the situation, we might close a larger wound with stitches but leave some gaps so that contamination is allowed to egress, or leak out from the wound. If you close the wound too tightly, it might trap bacteria in and cause a worse problem.

The other potential issue is rabies. What exactly is rabies? It is a virus that infects the nervous system and is almost always fatal once it causes symptoms in the brain. One of my favorite shows is *The Office* and one of my favorite episodes is the one about rabies, because they do a footrace to raise awareness for a cure for rabies after one of the characters is bitten by a bat. The episode makes the point that rabies has already been cured. If your child is bitten by a dog, you need to find out the vaccination status of the dog. Let the medical provider know the status. If you do not know the dog, try to find out who the owner is and ask them. Otherwise, the child may need to be administered the rabies vaccine. Rabies is also a concern with rodent bites. Foxes and bats also carry rabies commonly.

Chemical Contact and Burns

What if your child comes into contact with a chemical? There are a few general suggestions of what you should do. Remember that prevention is the major player in child safety for this issue.

Step 1: Remove the clothing and wash the child

If you witness the event or not, the best way to initially respond is to remove the child from the area of the spill, remove the child's clothing, including jewelry, watches, or other wearable items, and rinse them off as quickly as possible. Water is best[6], so do not worry about soap initially. There are certain chemicals that should not be washed with water or mixed with soap, and they include dry lime, elemental metals (pure sodium, for example), and phenol. Thankfully, you should not encounter these exceptions in your household as isolated compounds unless you have some weird hobbies. For most household compounds, water is the best place to start. Chemistry labs and other places may contain the above exceptions, but we are assuming a small child has been exposed to something in the house. Rinse the child with warm water with low pressure. Higher pressure can splash the chemical and contaminate other areas of the body, or even you. You can then proceed to use mild soap and/or a towel or dry brush to help remove the chemical. If the substance is a dry powder, brush it off first before using water. The solution to pollution is dilution.

Don't forget to protect yourself as well, depending on the chemical. Use gloves and a mask if available. Wear glasses as well so you don't splash your eyes.

Step 2: Beware of the eyes!

Children ages 1-2 are the highest risk of chemical burn to the eye.[7] If the eyes are contaminated or potentially contaminated, rinse thoroughly with water, with some recommendations stating as long as 15-30 minutes. If one eye is contaminated but the other isn't, be sure to cover the child's non-contaminated eye to prevent accidental spread. If you're dealing with an older child who wears contact lenses, the recommendation is to not remove the contact lens initially because it may protect the central portion of the eye. Instead, let a physician help.

Step 3: When to go to a Provider

Certainly, getting a small amount of shampoo or soap in the eye does not usually require a trip to the ED, but if you don't know what the chemical is, try to find the bottle with the label. The best instructions for how to deal with skin or eye contact are located on the package label. It will tell you the active and inactive ingredients and how to deal with the situation appropriately. While your child is rinsing in the shower, you can do an internet search for additional instructions if desired. If you do not know the compound, you should absolutely go the ED promptly after the initial rinse. For example, if your child gets into grandpa's storage shed and he keeps a bunch of unmarked old containers and your child gets into them, do an initial rinse with water and go to the ED.

Ingestion

I discussed ingestion in an earlier section, but I will address it here for quick reference. For material ingestion or suspected ingestion, call a provider or go to the nearest emergency setting, either an urgent care or emergency department. Remember, the biggest warning signs of partial blockage include:

- Trouble swallowing food
- Drooling
- Pain in the neck or chest
- Coughing
- Trouble breathing
- Noisy breathing

For chemical ingestion including medications, call a poison control center first. Their number is 1-800-222-1222. They can direct you on the appropriate next steps, including going to the nearest emergency care facility if necessary.

Other Plugs:

Stop the Bleed

Stop the Bleed® is a program sponsored by the American College of Surgeons, which is a professional organization of surgeons that provides education, advocacy, and research support. Stop the Bleed® also has the support of the U.S. Department of Defense. Stop the Bleed® started off as a program geared at teaching law enforcement agents to take care of victims in mass casualty events, specifically mass shootings or intentional actions of mass violence. The concept is prefaced on the fact that bleeding is the number one cause of preventable death after injury.[8] The first priority for law enforcement is to secure the scene after an event, and it can take quite a while until EMS or other first aid providers are allowed into the area. Victims could slowly bleed to death while waiting for them to arrive. By quickly stopping the bleeding with some simple and basic treatment, civilians already inside could potentially save lives.

The campaign has evolved to empower the general public to be able to respond to such situations. The program seeks to educate as many people as possible with strategies to stop bleedings and help victims prior to the arrival of medical providers on a scene, similar to how Basic Life Support (BLS) and Cardiopulmonary Resuscitation (CPR) classes are taught to educate bystanders how to help save lives.

The courses are typically 90 minutes in duration or less, and they teach you how to apply direct pressure to wounds, pack wounds, and use tourniquets safely. Most courses are free, and you can search on their website for local courses available to you. You can also contact your local hospital Emergency Department or EMS to see if they have classes available.

Discussions of mass casualties and mass shootings are outside the scope of this book, but I would recommend attending one of these classes similar to attending BLS course by the American Heart Association. You never know if your child could be endangered by a major trauma, such as a car accident or accidental gunshot, in which you would need to know how to control bleeding. It never hurts to be prepared!

In my home state, we are fortunate that the Georgia State Commission on Trauma, with support from the governor and funding from legislature, has made it a priority to educate most of the teachers and bus drivers in the state. Georgia also has funding to place 7 Stop the Bleed® kits in every public school in the state.

CitizenAID™

Another option for quick response to emergency situations is citizenAID™. This program was created by military and civilian medical providers to educate the general public on life saving first aid courses aimed at controlling bleeding in emergencies. According to their website, uncontrolled bleeding kills in 4 minutes or less.[9] They provide low-cost online courses that are approximately $14 as of April 2024. They also have a free app that you can download that walks you through what to do in emergency situations. If you are interested, download the free app now and not later, when it may be too late.

Again, this app and program are geared toward mass casualty events, such as bomb threats, knife attacks, active shooters, and vehicle attacks, but the lessons learned can be useful outside of just these events. I hope and pray that you will never need such skills, but you never know, and it never hurts to learn.

Bacteria vs. Viruses

Though I'm not going to write a textbook chapter on the subject, I would make many pediatricians happy if I discuss the differences between bacteria and viruses. Bacteria are single celled organisms that are capable of living and reproducing on their own. That means they contain the genetic material and the "machinery" capable of sustaining themselves and making more of themselves, though there are some caveats. Viruses, however, are not technically considered living organisms and can only be sustained by a host (the infected organism). They are also only capable of reproducing and multiplying by using host machinery rather than their own. The biology explanation of the differences is not as relevant to most parents, so let's get into something more relevant.

The main distinction that matters to parents and pediatricians is how you *treat* a bacterial infection versus a viral infection. Antibiotics work by either killing bacteria or keeping them from multiplying. They *do not* affect viruses in any way, shape, or form. Antivirals can affect certain viruses, but there are not antivirals available for most common viruses. The most common antiviral prescribed is called Tamiflu (generic name oseltamivir). It's used for the Influenza virus, or the flu. It's only effective if given within the first 48 hours of symptoms because it works by preventing the virus's ability to multiply. It does not work for any other virus.

Most common illnesses that affect children (and adults for that matter) are common viruses that do not have a specific antiviral or treatment. The treatment is to let your body fight the infection, or to "let it run its course." For many parents, the fact that a pediatrician does not prescribe an antibiotic is alarming. Rest assured that pediatricians are very well educated in how to treat pediatric infectious diseases and will make the right decision for treating your child. Not every illness requires an antibiotic.

Improper use of antibiotics can cause big issues, such as resistance. Resistance occurs when bacteria get exposed to an antibiotic in insufficient amounts so it can "learn" to be unaffected by the antibiotic. Therefore, the antibiotic may be completely ineffective against those bacteria in the future. This can occur on an individual level or on a population level. This means your specific bacteria you carry can become resistant, or the majority of the bacteria within a certain population can develop the resistance over time. This renders certain antibiotics potentially useless for bacteria that they used to be able to treat. As medical providers, we are taught to be good stewards of antibiotic use because the effects of overtreating can be extremely harmful to the worldwide community over time. How can you do your part as a patient or parent? If your child is prescribed an antibiotic, make sure your child takes the entire course and that you don't stop early just because the symptoms have gone away. The durations are prescribed for a reason, so complete them to keep resistance from building.

Strep throat is one of the most common bacterial issues that children face. This condition is best treated with antibiotics. Ear infections are often bacterial but can sometimes be treated without antibiotics depending on a few factors. The best way to deal with these issues as non-medical parents is to take your child to a pediatrician and trust them to make the right decision for your child. In fact, I do the same thing with my children. Though I have a crappy otoscope (the tool used to check ears), I learned long ago that I have a lot more peace in my marriage if my wife just takes the children to the pediatrician. I recommend you do the same if concerned.

***

References

1. David Skaggs MD, John Flynn MD, Peter Waters MD. *Rockwood and Wilkins' Fractures in Children*. 8th ed. Wolters Kluwer Health; 2015:1288.

2. Shaath K, Shirley E. Nursemaid's Elbow. Orthobullets. Updated August 21, 2022. Accessed September 25, 2024. https://www.orthobullets.com/pediatrics/4012/nursemaids-elbow#:~:text=Nursemaid's%20elbow%20is%20a%20common%20injury%20of%20early%20childhood%20that

3. Schutzman S. Minor blunt head trauma in infants and young children (<2 years): Clinical features and evaluation. UpToDate. Updated August 9, 2024. Accessed September 3, 2024. https://www.uptodate.com/contents/minor-blunt-head-trauma-in-infants-and-young-children-less-than2-years-clinical-features-and-evaluation?search=head%20injury%20pediatric&source=search_result&selectedTitle=2~150&usage_type=default&display_rank=2

4. Jasper J, Losh G. Evaluation and repair of tongue lacerations. UpToDate. Updated June 12, 2024. Accessed September 3, 2024. https://www.uptodate.com/contents/evaluation-and-repair-of-tongue-lacerations?search=tongue%20lacerations&source=search_result&selectedTitle=1~18&usage_type=default&display_rank=1

5. McTigue D, Azadani E. Evaluation and management of dental injuries in children. UpToDate. Updated April 18, 2023. Accessed

September 3, 2024. https://www.uptodate.com/contents/evaluation-and-management-of-dental-injuries-in-children?sectionName=Avulsions&search=tongue%20lacerations&topicRef=13876&anchor=H13&source=see_link#H13

6. Brent J. Water-based solutions are the best decontaminating fluids for dermal corrosive exposures: a mini review. *Clin Toxicol (Phila)*. Sep-Oct 2013;51(8):731-6. doi:10.3109/15563650.2013.838628

7. Haring RS, Sheffield ID, Channa R, Canner JK, Schneider EB. Epidemiologic Trends of Chemical Ocular Burns in the United States. *JAMA Ophthalmol*. Oct 1 2016;134(10):1119-1124. doi:10.1001/jamaophthalmol.2016.2645

8. STOP THE BLEED® Info. STOP THE BLEED. Accessed September 3, 2024. https://www.stopthebleed.org/frequently-asked-questions/

9. About citizenAID. Accessed September 25, 2024. https://citizenaid.us/about-us/

Chapter 22
Notes

Bare Bones

Jordan Paynter, MD

. . .

Bare Bones

Jordan Paynter, MD

. . .

Bare Bones

Stay Connected!

Check out our website at: www.barebonesdoc.com

Email us at: info@paynterbooks.com

Follow us on social media:

- Facebook: www.facebook.com/barebonesdoc
- Instagram: www.instagram.com/barebonesdoc
- Snapchat: www.snapchat.com/add/barebonesdoc
- X/Twitter: www.x.com/barebonesdoc
- Reddit: www.reddit.com/user/barebonesdoc
- Pinterest: www.pinterest.com/barebonesdoc
- TikTok: www.tiktok.com/@barebonesdoc
- YouTube: www.youtube.com/@barebonesdoc

Made in the USA
Columbia, SC
10 January 2025